Washington, D.C.
Off the Beaten Path®

Praise for the Off the Beaten Path® Series

"For the traveler who enjoys the special, the unusual, and the unexpected."

—*The Traveler* newsletter

"These well-researched, straightforward guides take travelers to popular spots as well as more obscure corners."

—*National Geographic Traveler*

Help Us Keep This Guide Up to Date

Every effort has been made by the author and editors to make this guide as accurate and useful as possible. However, many things can change after a guide is published—establishments close, phone numbers change, facilities come under new management, and so on.

We would love to hear from you concerning your experiences with this guide and how you feel it could be improved and kept up to date. Although we may not be able to respond to all comments and suggestions, we'll take them to heart and we'll also make certain to share them with the author. Please send your comments and suggestions to the following address:

The Globe Pequot Press
Reader Response/Editorial Department
P.O. Box 840
Guilford, CT 06437

Or you may e-mail us at:
editorial@globe-pequot.com

Thanks for your input, and happy travels!

Washington, D.C.

by William B. Whitman

The
Globe
Pequot
Press

Guilford, Connecticut

Cover photo is of the Bishop's Garden at the Washington National Cathedral, © by Alexandra K. Scott. (Alexandra Scott is photographer and co-author of *The Soul in Balance: The Gardens of Washington National Cathedral.*)
Cover and text design by Laura Augustine
Maps created by Equator Graphics; © The Globe Pequot Press
Illustrations by Carole Drong

Library of Congress Cataloging-in-Publication Data
Whitman, William B.
    Washington, D.C. : off the beaten path / by William B. Whitman. —1st ed.
      p. cm. —(Off the beaten path series)
    Includes index.
    ISBN 0-7627-0796-8
    1. Washington (D.C.)—Guidebooks. I. Title. II. Series.
    F192.3 . W48   2001
    917.5304'42—dc21   00-047611

Manufactured in the United States of America
First Edition/First Printing

*To Cameron, my patient wife, editorial assistant,
and boon companion from the District
to Dubrovnik and lots of places in-between.*

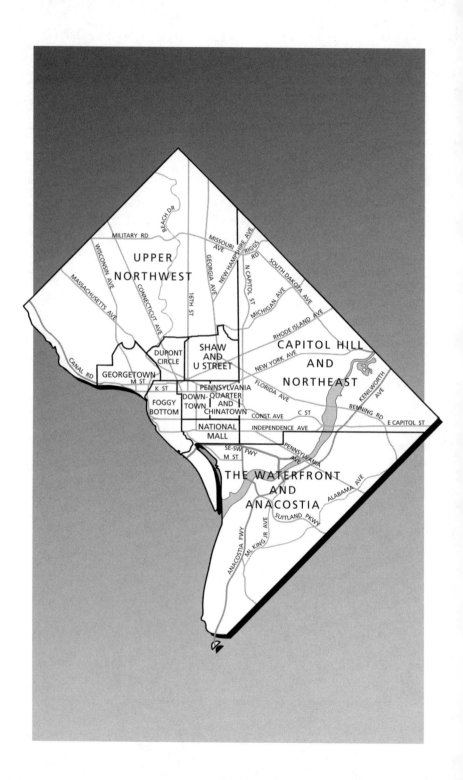

Contents

Acknowledgments

I'd like to thank my editors at The Globe Pequot Press, Laura Strom and Shelley Wolf, for their skillful help, sympathetic support, and occasional forbearance in making this guide a reality. Thanks also to friends who told me about their favorite off the beaten path places and to the Washington, D.C. Convention and Visitors Association, which provided valuable advice and information. And last but by no means least, let's not forget the D.C. Heritage Tourism Coalition, which, through its activities and its fascinating book, *Capital Assets,* is helping the District rediscover and rebuild the hidden places that contribute so much to its rich cultural fabric.

Introduction

Compared with Paris, London, Tokyo, and other world capitals, Washington is small in population and compact in size, but it offers travelers an extraordinary variety of visit choices. For example, tourists often follow well-worn paths to wander through Official Washington, which lines Pennsylvania Avenue from the White House to Capitol Hill, and, of course, Monumental Washington, the marble palaces of government and megamuseums that line the Mall from the Capitol to the Lincoln Memorial. It's only right that tourists and first-time visitors see the great symbols of our nation's heritage and democracy. But as the D.C. Heritage Tourism Coalition, which promotes visitor travel to Washington's vibrant neighborhoods, points out, "these sites are overcrowded . . . tourists are seeing only a fraction of what there is to see."

Tourists become travelers when they move off the Mall to explore Washington's historic neighborhoods to see great history, art, and culture without the crowds and packaging. This guide is aimed at taking you and other urban adventurers to Washington's secret places, where you'll visit often overlooked spots (some even in downtown Washington), that many visitors miss and most other guidebooks don't even mention. That's why you won't find the Capitol, the great Mall museums (including the Holocaust Museum and the National Gallery), and other much-visited attractions in this guide. What you will find are the city's hidden corners where you can explore art galleries, great architecture, world-class house museums, cultural landmarks, restaurants, and even shops that are indeed "off-the-beaten-path."

History

As you might have guessed, Washington became our capital as part of a political deal, in this case a 1790 trade-off of Southern congressional support for funding Northern state debts in exchange for moving the capital from Philadelphia to a southern location. George Washington determined that the new capital should be at the confluence of the

Potomac and Anacostia Rivers, between the thriving ports of Georgetown, Maryland, and Alexandria, Virginia. Washington hired a young
Frenchman, Pierre-Charles L'Enfant, who had been one of his staff officers at Valley Forge, to design the new capital. Peering down from the
hill that now holds Arlington Cemetery and Lee House at a rural valley
of woods and marshlands, L'Enfant saw instead a monumental city—
the "Territory of Columbia"—a dream capital with parks, canals, fountains, grand public buildings, and an orderly grid of north-south and
east-west streets overlaid by broad diagonal boulevards.

Getting Around

Although some of L'Enfant's original plans may have faded away, that
combination of a street grid and diagonal avenues, which now bear the
names of all fifty states, remains today, sometimes to the confusion of
visiting motorists trying to navigate the traffic circles at many of the
places where grid and diagonal intersect.

The grid itself is pretty simple: North-south streets are numbered;
east-west streets are lettered, starting with A, but there is no J, X, Y, or Z
Street. When the east-west grid runs out of single letters, it continues in
alphabetical order with two-syllable streets (Adams, Belmont, Channing,
and so on), until it reaches Windom or Yuma, after which it resumes in
alphabetical order with three-syllable names (Appleton, Brandywine,
and so on).

Washington is divided into four quadrants—Northeast (NE), Northwest
(NW), Southeast (SE), and Southwest (SW)—which converge at the
dome of the U.S. Capitol, the geographic center of Washington. The divid-
ing lines of those quadrants—North Capitol Street, East Capitol Street,
South Capitol Street, and the National Mall—radiate out from the Capitol. For example, an address with NW in its street name means the street is
north of the Mall and west of North Capitol Street. Pay careful attention to
the quadrant abbreviation that follows the street name; seemingly identi-
cal addresses can occur in all four quadrants, and you don't want to learn
the hard way that the corner of 17th Street and Pennsylvania Avenue NW
is a long, long way from that of 17th Street and Pennsylvania Avenue SE.

Transportation

Washington is blessed with an excellent, modern subway system called
Metrorail, which starts service at 5:30 A.M. weekdays and 8:00 A.M. on

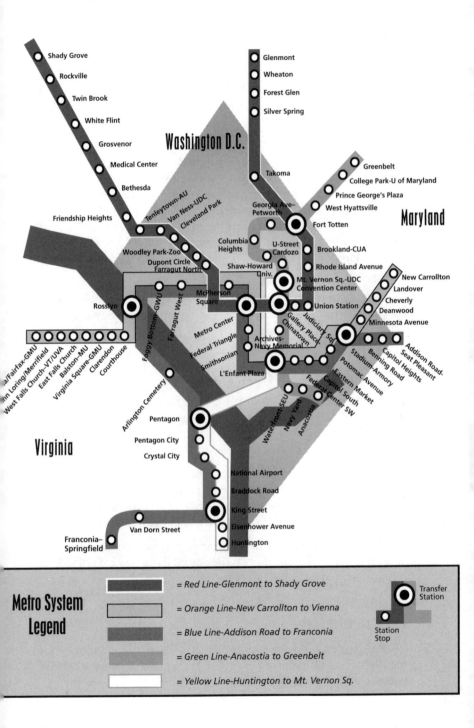

Shady Grove
Rockville
Twin Brook
White Flint
Grosvenor
Medical Center
Bethesda
Friendship Heights

Washington D.C.

Glenmont
Wheaton
Forest Glen
Silver Spring

Takoma

Greenbelt
College Park-U of Maryland
Prince George's Plaza
West Hyattsville
Georgia Ave–Petworth
Fort Totten

Maryland

Tenleytown-AU
Van Ness-UDC
Cleveland Park

Columbia Heights
U-Street Cardozo
Shaw-Howard Univ.

Brookland-CUA
Rhode Island Avenue

Woodley Park-Zoo
Dupont Circle
Farragut North

Mt. Vernon Sq.-UDC
Convention Center

New Carrollton
Landover
Cheverly
Deanwood
Minnesota Avenue

Rosslyn

Foggy Bottom-GWU
Farragut West

McPherson Square

Metro Center

Union Station

Judiciary Sq.
Gallery Place-Chinatown

Addison Road-Seat Pleasant
Capitol Heights
Benning Road

Vienna/Fairfax-GMU
Dunn Loring/Merrifield
West Falls Church-VT/UVA
East Falls Church
Balston-MU
Virginia Square-GMU
Clarendon
Courthouse

Federal Triangle
Archives-Navy Memorial
Smithsonian
L'Enfant Plaza

Stadium-Armory
Potomac Avenue
Eastern Market
Capitol South
Federal Center SW

Arlington Cemetery

Pentagon
Pentagon City
Crystal City

Virginia

Waterfront-SEU
Navy Yard
Anacostia

National Airport
Braddock Road
King Street
Eisenhower Avenue
Huntington

Franconia–Springfield

Van Dorn Street

Metro System Legend

= Red Line-Glenmont to Shady Grove

= Orange Line-New Carrollton to Vienna

= Blue Line-Addison Road to Franconia

= Green Line-Anacostia to Greenbelt

= Yellow Line-Huntington to Mt. Vernon Sq.

Transfer Station

Station Stop

weekends. It closes at midnight, except on Saturday and Sunday when the witching hour is 1:00 A.M.

Metro fares range from $1.10 to $3.25, depending on the length of the ride and the time of day (rush hour fares are more expensive). You can also buy one-day passes for unlimited travel for $5.00, and there's a seven-day pass for $25.00.

Because Metro is fast, reliable, and safe, it is usually the best way to get around the city. The attractions in this guide are often, but not always, keyed to Metro travel and the name of the nearest stop. Because Washington traffic is heavy and parking is expensive, you'd be well advised to give your jalopy a rest and take public transport. When Metrorail is not feasible, there's a good chance that the city's excellent Metrobus system will get you there, and the appropriate route will be given. For more information about Washington's public transit system, go to www.wmata.com or call 637–7000.

Taxis are plentiful and relatively inexpensive, so they are another useful option for getting around, especially in unfamiliar or edgy neighborhoods.

Fees, Prices, and Rates

The good news is that most of Washington's great attractions, both on and off the beaten path, are free. In fact, sightseeing in the nation's capital is a freeloader's dream. Unless this guide mentions an admission fee, you can assume that there isn't one.

Restaurants and lodgings are another matter. Washington consistently ranks as one of America's most expensive cities. This guide will give you an indication of what you can expect to pay for meals: under $15 is considered inexpensive, $15 to $35 is moderate, and $35 and up is expensive.

When it comes to lodgings (a standard double, excluding the District's 13% room tax), $125 and under is considered inexpensive, $125 to $225 is moderate, and $225 and up is expensive.

Area Code

Washington's one and only area code is 202. When calling from outside the District, all of the phone numbers in this book (unless otherwise noted) can be reached by using the 202 prefix.

Sources of Info

After you arrive, you'll have several excellent sources for news of what's happening while you're in Washington:

The *Washington Post* (www.washingtonpost.com) is a great national newspaper, but it also pays close attention to its home town. The daily Metro and Style sections are prime sources of news about what's going on, while the Friday *Weekend* magazine always carries an extensive listing of cultural and other events of the moment.

Washington City Paper (www.washingtoncitypaper.com), widely distributed everywhere (and free!), carries an exhaustive compilation of tours, concerts, and museum happenings, along with highly professional exposés about what's really going on in D.C. Even if you're just hanging out and not thinking much about culture, *City Paper* is for you.

The *Washingtonian* (www.washingtonian.com), the city's local magazine, is very strong on gallery schedules, details about what's happening at local museums, and superb restaurant coverage. Pick one up for both operational information and a good feel for what Washington is all about.

If you've arrived by air you've surely seen *Washington Flyer* (www.fly2dc. com), which is widely circulated at Dulles and National airports. Unlike the usual airport freebie publications, *Flyer* is a magazine with heft and content that will help you get around very nicely, from its front-of-the-book articles on local attractions to its listings of Washington sights, museum happenings, and restaurants. Best of all, *Washington Flyer* regularly covers off-the-beaten-path places like the ones you're going to see.

Visitor information is available from the Washington Convention and Visitors Association, 1212 New York Avenue NW (789–7000, www. washington.org) and the D. C. Chamber of Commerce Visitor Information Center, Ronald Reagan Building, 1300 Pennsylvania Avenue NW (first floor, east side); 328–4748. Open daily 8:00 A.M. to 6:00 P.M.

Tour Groups and Organizers

Although there's no shortage of trolley and bus tours to take you to the usual sites, off-the-beaten-path exploration requires more specific and close-up help, ideally a walking tour with a knowledgeable guide. Here are a few to consider, along with a specialized possibility or two:

Beyond the Monuments is operated by the D.C. Heritage Tourism Coalition, which is dedicated to promoting the tourist potential of Washington's historic neighborhoods. This useful service provides one-stop shopping for clear, detailed information about how to hook up with professionally led walking tours of each area covered in this book. Just call 828–WALK and select the part of the city you're interested in. All tours are of the walk-up variety and leave from Metro stations. The D.C. Heritage Web site, www.dcheritage.com, has more information.

Anecdotal History Tours. Every Sunday from 11:00 A.M. to 1:00 P.M., tour guide Anthony Pitch takes a group to some of D.C.'s hidden corners. The rotating list includes Georgetown, Around the White House, White House to the Capitol, and Adams Morgan. For a schedule, call (301) 294–9514 or go to www.dcsightseeing.com. Cost is $10 per person. Groups by appointment.

Bike the Sites. Daily three-hour guided bike tours follow paths and trails to visit a number of sites in the District, including Capitol Hill and Georgetown. The $35 price includes bike rental, entrance fees, and snack. Tours can be arranged for small groups, so think about family touring. Visit www.bikethesites.com on-line or call 966–8662.

Tour D.C offers highly knowledgeable ninety-minute walking tours of Georgetown every Saturday and Thursday at 10:30 A.M. Also tours of Dupont Circle and other neighborhoods. Call (301) 588–8999 for details.

Washington Walks has a selection of about ten possibilities for walks through a number of places in this book, plus a "Capital Hauntings" tour to some of the city's ghostly places. Each walk starts at a Metro station, lasts two hours, and costs $10 per person. For details, call 484–1565 or check out www.washingtonwalks.com.

Annual Events

Washington has literally hundreds of special events every year, but listed here are a few of the city's leading festivals, shows, and special tours. Because the dates for many of these occasions vary from year to year, you'll also find a phone number or Web site where you can find exact dates and more information. The *Washington Post* and *City Paper* are also excellent sources for the latest about these and other major events.

January

Martin Luther King Jr. Birthday Celebration. Performances, exhibits, and readings commemorate the life and legacy of the human rights leader. 789–7029.

February

Black History Month at the Smithsonian. Monthlong exhibitions and activities reflecting African-American history and culture. 357–2700.

Chinese Lunar New Year Parade. Chinatown parade plus fireworks, dragon dancers, and lion dancers. 638–1041.

Washington Boat Show. Hundreds of boats ranging from dinghies to motor yachts. (703) 823–7960.

Abraham Lincoln's Birthday Celebration. Reading of the Gettysburg Address at the Lincoln Memorial. 619–7222.

Frederick Douglass Birthday. Frederick Douglass National Historic Site. 426–5961.

> ### Capital Quote
>
> *"Wherever else an American citizen may be a stranger, he should be at home in his nation's capital."*
>
> —*Frederick Douglass, 1877*

March

St. Patrick's Day Parade. Thousands cheer along Constitution Avenue as the Irish march, the dancers dance, and the bagpipes play. (301) 879–1717.

Smithsonian's Annual Kite Festival. Held the last Saturday in March at the Washington Monument. 357–2700.

Late March or early April

Cherry Blossom Parade and Festival. Thousands of cherry blossoms, a parade, and a Festival Queen to boot. For tickets, call 432–SEAT. For details, call the Festival Committee at 547–1500.

Washington Flower and Garden Show. Display gardens with thousands of flowers and trees, and they are all in full bloom. (703) 823–7960.

April

White House Spring Garden Tour. See the great White House gardens while military bands serenade. 208–1631.

Annual White House Easter Egg Roll. Children ages three to six gather on the White House South Lawn; older children roll their eggs on the Ellipse. Eggs and live entertainment are provided and, just maybe, an appearance by the President. 208–1631 or 456–2322.

Smithsonian Craft Show. More than 100 leading American artisans display and sell their textiles, ceramics, wood, metal, and glass. 357–2700.

Georgetown House Tour. One weekend each spring private homes are open to the public. 338–1796.

May

Georgetown Garden Day. A self-guided walking tour of dozens of beautiful gardens. 333–3921.

The National Cathedral Flower Mart. Flower booths, crafts and demonstrations, held the first weekend in May. 537–6200, www.cathe dral.org.

Annual Goodwill Embassy Tour. On the second Saturday in May, embassies open their doors to the public. 636–4225.

Annual Candlelight Vigil Ceremony. National Law Enforcement Officers Memorial. 737–3400.

Memorial Day Weekend Concerts. The National Symphony Orchestra performs on the West Lawn of the Capitol. 619–7222.

Memorial Day Ceremonies. Arlington National Cemetery (685–2851), Vietnam Veterans Memorial (619–7222), and the U.S. Navy Memorial (737–2300).

May—August

Twilight Tattoo. Every Wednesday from early May until early August, the U.S. Army Military District of Washington stages a stirring sunset parade on the Ellipse, south of the White House. 685–4989.

June

Dupont-Kalorama Museum Walk Weekend. Visits to six neighborhood museums and historic houses. 667–0441.

Shakespeare Theatre Free for All. Carter Barron Amphitheatre. An annual festival put on by the Shakespeare Theatre in Rock Creek Park's Carter Barron Amphitheatre. 547–3230.

Smithsonian's Festival of American Folklife. This annual festival of food, crafts, music, and dance is held on the National Mall and runs until July 4. 357–2700.

June–August

Marine Band Summer Concert Series. Wednesday at 8:00 P.M. at the U.S. Capitol and Sunday at 7:00 P.M. on the Mall. 433–4011.

U.S. Army Band Summer Concert Series. Thursday at 8:00 P.M. on the steps of the U.S. Capitol. 685–2851, www.army.mil/armyband.

July

National Independence Day Celebration. Day-long concerts, a morning parade, and the famed evening entertainment on the National Mall. 619–7222.

Soap Box Derby. Independence day race on Constitution Avenue. 237–7200.

Bastille Day. Always ready for a party, Washington celebrates French Independence Day with live entertainment and a race to the U.S. Capitol and back by tray-bearing waiters and waitresses. 296–7200.

September

National Symphony Orchestra's Labor Day Concert. West Lawn of the U.S. Capitol. 619–7222.

Black Family Reunion. The annual celebration of the African-American family features live entertainment, food, and pavilions. 737–0120.

Kennedy Center Open House. Free concerts and performances. 467–4600.

National Cathedral Open House. Cathedral-related music, tours, tower climbs, and entertainment. 537–6200.

September–October

Hispanic Heritage Month. The Smithsonian hosts a month of arts, entertainment, and educational activities celebrating Hispanic culture and traditions. 357–2700, www.si.edu.

October

Taste of D.C. Festival. Pennsylvania Avenue is lined with stands offering foods from forty of D.C.'s hottest restaurants. Live entertainment too. 724–5430.

White House Fall Garden and House Tours. Visit the White House gardens and public rooms while military bands entertain. 208–1631 or 456–2322.

Marine Corps Marathon. Thousands run in this annual marathon from the Iwo Jima Memorial in Arlington to the Capitol and back. Applications available February 1. (703) 784–2225, www.marinemarathon.com.

Washington International Horse Show. One of the East's premiere shows, where hunting and jumping horses compete for prizes. (301) 840–0281.

November

American Indian Heritage Month. The Smithsonian celebrates with special programs and exhibitions. 357–2700.

Veterans Day Ceremonies. Arlington National Cemetery (685–2951), the Vietnam Veterans Memorial (619–7222), and Navy Memorial (737–2300).

December

Kennedy Center Holiday Festival. Free performances and holiday concerts all month. 467– 4600.

National Cathedral Christmas Services. A month of pageants, carols, and choruses. 619– 7222.

National Christmas Tree Lighting Pageant of Peace. Get to the Ellipse early for the 5:00 P.M. ceremony at which the president lights the national Christmas tree. From then until New Year's Day, the Ellipse is the site of nightly choral performances. 208–1631 or 619–7222.

The Washington Ballet's *The Nutcracker.* A Washington holiday tradition. 432–SEAT.

White House Christmas Candlelight Tours. Evening tours of the White House, its Christmas decorations, and holiday candlelight. 208–1631 or 456–2322.

The prices and rates listed in this guidebook were confirmed at press time. We recommend, however, that before traveling, you call establishments to obtain current information.

Downtown

ike the rings of a great tree, Washington's buildings and public spaces trace the American past, from the outer layers of Watergate and the Vietnam Memorial down to the innermost bands of pre-Revolutionary Georgetown and the Marine Barracks. But the city's core has always been the White House, more modest by far than the mansions occupied by heads of state in many less affluent or powerful countries, but for more than 200 years the symbol of America all over the planet. Thousands of tourists pour through the Executive Mansion every year before following well-worn paths to the next attraction, but more inquisitive travelers with historic perspectives think of the White House in its original role as the center of an old Washington neighborhood. Start exploring the President's neighborhood in *Lafayette Square,* which was the Pierce family farm, orchard, and burial ground when L'Enfant's plan projected it as the President's Park, where the Chief Executive could relax and seek relief from the capital's sizzling summers.

It may have been named for the Revolutionary War hero the Marquis de Lafayette, but the Square really belongs to Andrew Jackson, starting with the Spanish cannon captured by Old Hickory at Pensacola to the statue of Jackson on a capering horse, as Henry James put it, "as archaic as a Ninevite king, prancing and rocking through the ages." Jackson's statue looks down on the scene of his notorious 1829 inaugural, when tubs of whiskey and high-octane orange punch were rolled into the square to lure the drunken, coonskin-capped crowds out of the White House, touching off a wild melee that prompted the Chief Justice to sniff that "the reign of King Mob seemed triumphant."

The Square has also seen military service, when soldiers bivouacked there, first during the War of 1812 and again during the Civil War, turning it both times into a muddy swamp. President Grant later used it as his private zoo until the aroma of the presidential prairie dogs became intolerable.

But the Square's most distinctive and enduring role was as the social headquarters of antebellum Washington, a time when, as Square-dweller Henry Adams recalled, "beyond the square the country began."

Downtown

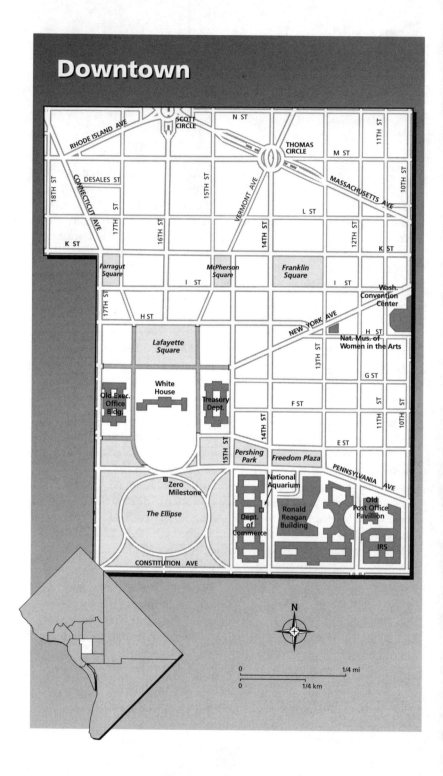

DOWNTOWN

TOP ATTRACTIONS IN DOWNTOWN

Treasury Building

National Geographic Society

Old Executive Office Building

Renwick Gallery

Decatur House

National Museum of Women in the Arts

National Theater

B'nai B'rith National Jewish Museum

Old Post Office Pavilion Observation Deck

President and Mrs. Kennedy rescued many of the Square's elegant town houses from demolition in the 1960s, when the so-called planners saw this as the place for a government office complex.

On your stroll along the east side of the Square you'll pass the **Tayloe House** at number 721 Madison Place, a Federal beauty with an iron-work balcony that was known as "The Little White House" when it was the home of Mark Hanna, President McKinley's éminence grise. The widowed Dolley Madison lived in the Madison-Cutts House, where the Square meets H Street, until her death in 1849. During the Civil War the house belonged to General George McClellan, who, one night in November 1862, deliberately snubbed Abraham Lincoln. After waiting an hour in the parlor to see the absent general, the president was told that McClellan had in the meantime returned but had gone to bed.

At the top of the square stands St. John's Episcopal Church, "the church of the presidents," where every president since Madison has worshiped in pew 54. The parish house next door is Ashburton House, which was the British legation in the 1840s.

At the corner of H Street and Jackson Place, visitors get a crash course on the history of Washington social life. Capital insiders have gathered for almost two centuries at **Decatur House,** built in 1819 by Commodore Stephen Decatur, the swashbuckling hero of the War of 1812, with prize money earned from his naval victories. His Federal town house soon became one of the young capital's social and power centers, but not for long; a year later Decatur was mortally wounded in a duel. Decatur House then became the residence of three Secretaries of State: Martin Van Buren, Edward Livingston, and Henry Clay, who bragged (correctly) that he was "living in the best home of the city."

In the house's downstairs rooms you'd swear that the Decaturs had just stepped out, perhaps to pay a call on President Monroe just across the park. On the gleaming eighteenth-century desk in the Commodore's office, documents are ready for his signature, while in the parlor the needlepoint and decoupage strewn on the couch tell us that Susan Decatur took an interest in what guys back in 1819 used to call "women's pastimes." In the stately dining room, a table set with Chinese export porcelain awaits the Decaturs' return.

Capital Quote

"Washington talks about herself, and about almost nothing else. It is about herself as the City of Conversation that she incessantly converses."

—Henry James

But on the second floor, visitors enter a time warp and fast-forward to the end of the nineteenth century and the Victorian tastes of the socially prominent Beale family, who lived here from 1871 to 1957. In these upstairs parlors, where the Decaturs entertained at "crushes" and "squeezes"—the 1820 ancestors of the infamous Washington cocktail party—the Beales entertained in late nineteenth century grandeur amid an eclectic collection of furnishings, ranging from delicate Japanese screens to ornate Belter-style American pieces of dark woods and red velvets. And in the center of the dining room floor the Beales placed a seal of California inlaid in rare woods to remind them of the source of the family ranching fortune.

Wandering through all this Victoriana, there's yet another time shift when you hear the voices of Kate Smith and Glenn Miller drifting from the restored office of social doyenne Marie Beale, whose Bakelite radio brings back memories of 1944. On the desk you'll see a vintage Royal typewriter and copies of *Life* magazines recounting Mrs. Beale's glittering wartime parties in these very rooms. Decatur House, at 748 Jackson Place NW (842–0920, www.decaturhouse.org), is open 10:00 A.M. to 3:00 P.M. Tuesday through Friday, noon to 4:00 P.M. Saturday and Sunday. Guided tours are given every half hour; the last one begins at 2:30 P.M. Admission is $4.00 for adults, $2.50 for students and seniors, free for members of the National Trust for Historic Preservation. The House's excellent gift shop, located in the former slave quarters, is open Monday through Friday 10:00 A.M. to 5:00 P.M., weekends noon to 4:00 P.M. Decatur House is the only Lafayette Square home open to the public. Metro: Farragut West (orange and blue lines).

Before you leave the Square be sure to visit each corner to inspect the statues of foreign heroes of the Revolution: de Rochambeau, Kosciusko, von Steuben, and Lafayette himself at the southeast corner.

Near the corner where Lafayette Square meets Pennsylvania Avenue, you'll find another famous house—well, actually two. One, Blair House, was built in 1824 by the aristocratic Blairs of Maryland, while the Lee House next door belonged to the aristocratic Lees of Virginia; this is where Robert E. Lee was offered command of the Union Army and, as a loyal Virginian, refused. The merger of the two houses is now known officially as ***Blair House,*** where Presidents put up visiting heads of state. The tradition began during World War II, when Eleanor Roosevelt wearied of having houseguest Winston Churchill padding around the White House

AUTHOR'S FAVORITES IN DOWNTOWN

Old Executive Office Building

Lafayette Square and Decatur House

Chapters Bookstore

Treasury Department

The Palm

in his Doctor Dentons, a brandy glass in hand. (You would have too.) In 1950, when Harry Truman was living there while the White House was being reconstructed, Puerto Rican nationalists stormed Blair House in an assassination attempt. A plaque on the Blair House fence honors the bravery of Secret Service agent Leslie Coffelt, who was shot and killed defending the president. Blair House is not open to the public. Metro: Farragut West (orange and blue lines).

Next door to Blair House, the **Renwick Gallery** exhibits the best in American arts, crafts, and design. Its gingerbread building was designed by James Renwick (also the architect of the Smithsonian "castle" on the National Mall) to hold the art collection of local banker William Corcoran. Alas, Mr. Corcoran's new toy was completed in 1861, just in time to be seized by the government and used as a warehouse for Army uniforms; when it reopened in 1869 it became Washington's first art museum. When the Corcoran collection moved down 17th Street (see the Foggy Bottom chapter) in 1897, this became the U.S. Court of Claims building until 1964, when it was transferred to the Smithsonian.

After ascending the Renwick's imposing staircase, just as President Grant did at the gala ball that reopened Corcoran's collection, you'll find the gallery's permanent exhibits of furniture, glassware, and textiles, a nice combination of the traditional and contemporary.

But prepare to be overwhelmed by the sumptuous "Grand Salon" at the top of the stairs. It's always the Gilded Age in this grand, almost overwhelming room, where dozens of great paintings from every era of American history are beautifully hung, salon-style, on high silk-covered walls. Among the most memorable are the George Catlins, with fabulous scenes of the West in the 1830s and portraits of great warrior chiefs in full war dress. The Salon also has some rare pieces by California artist Hugo Ballin, and two Albert Henderson Thayer portraits of his children and family. The Renwick Gallery, at Pennsylvania Avenue and 17th Street (357–2531, www.americanart.si.edu), is open from 10:00 A.M. to 5:30 P.M. every day. Metro: Farragut West (blue and orange lines) and Farragut North (red line).

Across Pennsylvania Avenue looms the **Old Executive Office Building,** another ornate Victorian that somehow manages to be both highly visible and rarely visited. Tourists and Washingtonians hurrying along Pennsylvania Avenue never fail to gaze in wonderment at this massive

Renwick Gallery

granite ziggurat next door to the White House, but few realize that behind that operatic facade bristling with columns, pilasters, and porticoes lies a bygone world where graceful stairways, exquisite architectural details, and elegant rooms exude both refinement and power.

A visit to the Old Executive Office Building (OEOB to its friends) is a must for anyone interested in American design, politics, and history. This Victorian dowager has been the ground zero of American strength and decision-making since the day it opened in 1875, when it accommodated three entire government departments: State, War, and Navy. Several presidents, including both Roosevelts, Eisenhower, and Taft, worked here before moving next door to 1600 Pennsylvania, while twenty-five secretaries of state have had their offices in the south wing overlooking the Ellipse. The west wing, which once housed the War Department, has its own memories of George C. Marshall, Douglas MacArthur, and Major Dwight D. Eisenhower. Although the three original agencies left long ago, OEOB is still the home of the powerful, whose list of tenants includes the vice president and the chairmen of both the Council of Economic Advisors and the National Security Council, where Ollie North and his sidekick, Fawn Hall, shredded the Iran-Contra documents.

Members of the regular Saturday morning tour of OEOB follow high-ceilinged hallways to explore hidden treasures like the Indian Treaty Room, a jewel box of brightly tiled floors and wrought iron balconies where presidents since Harry Truman have held press conferences. Another visitor favorite is room 274, once the office of Franklin Roosevelt and other secretaries of the Navy and now the ceremonial office of the vice president, where marble fireplaces, gleaming marquetry floors, and gold-framed mirrors epitomize Victorian elegance. Other stops include the former State Department library, with three stories of lacy white and gold railings, a ceiling of filigreed glass, and a floor of antique Minton tile. You'll be impressed by the wealth of architectural craftsmanship on the tour, including grand staircases that swoop up to coffered domes and stained glass rotundas, and details such as intricately cast doorknobs and trash chutes.

Old Executive Office Building

Although security considerations rule out casual strolls around the OEOB, look for some special places in a building where every office has a history. In room 208, on the morning of December 7, 1941, Secretary of State Cordell Hull received then ejected Japan's emissaries. Room 488 was once the top secret "black room," where American cryptographers broke enemy codes.

Saturday tours of the Old Executive Office Building, at 17th Street and Pennsylvania Avenue, must be reserved in advance by calling 395–5895 between 9:00 A.M. and noon Tuesday through Friday. When booking you must provide the date of birth and social security number for each visitor and you will need a photo ID when you arrive for the tour. To get a preview, visit the OEOB Web site at www.whitehouse.gov/wh/tours/oeob. Metro: Farragut West (blue and orange lines) and Farragut North (red line).

You'll find one of D.C.'s best-kept secrets at 1500 Pennsylvania Avenue, a.k.a. the ***Treasury Department,*** where Saturday tour members walk directly from a busy twentieth-century street into the Treasury Department of 1842. The austerity of these Tyler Administration corridors of power, with their cast-iron columns and graceful stairways, seem to embody the spartan tastes of a young, egalitarian republic, that is, until your guide takes you behind those louvered office doors into the suite used by Treasury Secretary Salmon P. Chase during the Civil War, where the simple gives way to the sumptuous.

Everything in these handsome offices—the decoratively stenciled ceilings with allegorical themes, the fireplace with its mammoth over-mantel mirror, and the glossy leather furniture—has been meticulously restored to reflect the days when Lincoln ambled over from the White House to anguish with Chase about finding ways to finance the war effort. Don't let this spoil your tour, but these splendid rooms are the birthplace of the income tax, first levied in 1862 to raise money for the Union cause.

Just after Lincoln's assassination, the Andrew Johnson Suite down the hall was turned into Johnson's Oval Office, where, as vintage prints show, the new president conducted his first cabinet meetings and received foreign funeral delegations. In the office next door, which once belonged to the Secretary of the Treasury and is now used by a senior department official, computers and printers coexist nicely with the massive conference tables, richly upholstered chairs, and thick drapes of 1875.

Treasury architect Alfred Mullett wanted the building's Cash Room to be "emblematic of the dignity of the nation and the stability of its credit," so he designed it as an Italian palazzo, its two-story walls covered with colored marble and ringed by a balcony with exquisitely wrought bronze railings. Immense gaslight chandeliers look down on the banking floor where tellers once sold bonds, cashed government checks, and redeemed banknotes with silver and gold hauled from the currency and bullion vaults just below.

Although it was called "the most expensive room in the world" when it opened, the Cash Room started off with a social calamity: At Grant's 1869 Inaugural Reception, hungry guests stampeded the kitchen, women fainted in the crush, and the search for coats went on all night. Be glad you weren't invited.

Treasury Department tours last ninety minutes and start at the visitor area inside the building's 15th Street entrance on Saturday mornings at 10:00, 10:20, 10:40, and 11:00. Reservations are essential and must be made at least three days in advance by calling 622–0896 or 622–0692. For security reasons you'll also need a picture ID. Children under twelve

Mayflower Madam

are not admitted. Note: If you take the 9:00 A.M. OEOB tour and hustle down Pennsylvania Avenue, you'll be able to make the 11:00 A.M. Treasury tour. Metro: Metro Center (red, orange, and blue lines).

Dressed in basic black (no pearls), FBI Director J. Edgar Hoover lunched at the same table at the Mayflower Hotel every day for twenty years.

The *National Museum of Women in the Arts* is probably the only museum anywhere dedicated to the achievements of women in every area of the arts. Its large and thoughtfully assembled permanent collection showcases women's achievements over five centuries, beginning with rare portraits by two of the few women painters of the Italian renaissance, Sofonisba Anguissola and Lavinia Fontana. The exhibit continues chronologically through Mary Cassatt right down to the vibrant oils of contemporary artists; the museum also regularly hosts special traveling exhibits. Oddly enough, the museum is located in what was once one of the ultimate boys' clubs, a handsome Renaissance Revival building erected in 1908 as Washington's Masonic Temple. The knockout entrance hall exhibit area dates from its later days as a 1930s movie palace. Adding to the abundance, the fine museum shop is dedicated to books, images, and posters by women

Red Meat Department

*W*ashington opened the twenty-first century with a stampede of New York steak houses. The venerable Palm, always a White House–media clubhouse and hangout for local movers and shakers, was joined by fellow New Yorkers Smith and Wollensky, Bobby Van's Steakhouse, and Maloney and Porcelli. So for a thick steak or mammoth lobster, here's what you need to know; just don't tell your cardiologist:

- *The Palm,* 1225 19th Street NW (293–9091), is open Monday through Friday 11:45 A.M. to 10:00 P.M., Saturday and Sunday 6:00 to 10:30 P.M. Expensive. Located downtown.

- *Maloney and Porcelli,* 601 Indiana Avenue NW (478–8300), is open

Monday through Friday 11:30 A.M. to 11:30 P.M., Saturday and Sunday 5:00 to 11:30 P.M. Expensive. Located in the Pennsylvania Quarter.

- *Smith and Wollensky,* 1112 19th Street NW (466–1100), is open Monday through Friday 11:30 A.M. to 4:00 P.M. and 5:00 to 11:00 P.M., Saturday and Sunday 5:00 to 11:00 P.M. Upstairs grill room open 11:30 A.M. to 2:00 A.M. every day. Expensive. Located downtown.

- *Bobby Van's Steakhouse,* 809 15th Street NW (589–0060), is open Monday through Friday 11:30 A.M. to 10:00 P.M., Saturday and Sunday 4:00 to 10:00 P.M. Expensive. Located downtown.

The Zero Milestone

All distances within the United States to Washington are measured from that oblong milestone on the Ellipse directly behind the White House.

artists and photographers. The museum, at 1250 New York Avenue NW, is open Monday through Saturday 10:00 A.M. to 5:00 P.M. and Sunday from noon to 5:00 P.M. Voluntary contribution. Call 783–5000 or (800) 222–7270, fax 393–3234, or visit www.nmwa. org. Metro: Metro Center (red, blue, and orange lines).

The **National Theatre,** where greats like Helen Hayes, John Barrymore, and Sarah Bernhardt once performed, has been part of America's theatrical tradition since 1835. On a nonperfoming level, Shirley McLaine and her brother, Warren Beatty, worked as usher and stage doorman, respectively, in the 1950s.

The current theater, at 1321 Pennsylvania Avenue NW, is the fifth edition of the National on this site. Like the Paris Opera, the National also has its very own phantom, the occasionally spotted ghost of John McCullough, a prominent actor of the 1880s who was murdered precisely where the present-day stage is located.

The National is still very much a prominent part of Washington's cultural scene and regularly hosts many pre- and post-Broadway performances, but three much less publicized (and free) presentations are also on the National's regular schedule. Every Monday at 6:00 and 7:30 P.M. from September to May, "Monday Night at the National," features mainly local performers in plays, readings, and performances of dance and music. "Saturday Morning at the National," a children's program that often includes storytellers and puppets, is presented each Saturday from September to May at 9:30 and 11:30 A.M. Every Monday at 6:30 P.M. from June through August, the National hosts a "Summer Cinema Program" of classic films.

Although these events are free, you'll still need tickets to get in. To get them, on a first-come first-served basis, turn up at the box office at least thirty minutes prior to the performance. For information about these and any other performances (or if you run into Mr. McCullough), call 626–6161. Metro: Federal Triangle (orange and blue lines).

When it opened in 1997, the **Ronald Reagan Building and International Trade Center,** named for the president who strongly favored a massive rollback in the bureaucracy, became the second largest Federal office building in the United States, surpassed in floor space only by the Pentagon. The ultimate paradox? Two of its major tenants are agencies The Gipper had sworn to eliminate. Anyway, just because it's full of feds, don't pass up a chance to peer inside this massive structure at the corner

Peace Corps Gift Shop

*T*ucked away in the Peace Corps headquarters building at 1111 20th Street NW, this little gem escaped everyone's attention until Bill and Hillary did their Christmas shopping there. You too can buy the shop's CDs, with music from many of the nations hosting Peace Corps programs, or an assortment of masks, textiles, and other artifacts volunteers have brought back from their assignments. Across the lobby there's an exhibit of Peace Corps history. Open Monday through Friday from 9:00 A.M. to 5:00 P.M. Call 872–8101. Metro: Foggy Bottom–GWU or Farragut West (orange and blue lines).

of 13th Street and Pennsylvania Avenue NW. Once beyond that ostentatious facade, visitors gaze out over a stunning atrium used for special occasions and regular art exhibits. The Reagan building is open weekdays from 7:00 A.M. to 7:00 P.M., and 11:00 A.M. to 7:00 P.M. on Saturday. Free tours of the building start from the concierge desk at the 14th Street entrance every Monday, Wednesday, and Friday at 11:00 A.M. The building's well-stocked visitor information center with interactive tours of the city and tickets for real tours (328–7748) is open Monday through Saturday 8:00 A.M. to 6:00 P.M.

The Reagan building also contains a large food court as well as **Palomino,** a handsome two-level restaurant with an impressive but reasonably priced "euro-bistro" lunch menu. Palomino, reachable at 842–9800, is open daily 11:30 A.M. to 3:00 P.M., and 5:00 to 11:00 P.M. Moderate. Metro: Federal Triangle (orange and blue lines).

See vicious sharks dining on the lower end of the food chain! Thrill to razor-toothed piranha fighting for their seafood dinner! Are we somewhere along the Amazon or on a Pacific reef? Not at all; we're in the basement of an utterly prosaic government building, where most of the infighting goes on upstairs in offices and not downstairs in fish tanks. The **National Aquarium,** on the lower level of the Commerce Department Building at 14th Street and Constitution Avenue NW, has seventy tanks teeming with every form of aquatic life, including sea turtles, alligators, and tropical fish; the shark and piranha feedings, however, are the biggest draw. To see why, go there Monday, Wednesday, or Saturday at 2:00 P.M. to watch the sharks get a late lunch; the piranha dine at 2:00 P.M. on Tuesday, Thursday, and Sunday. Keep a close eye on the kids! Fortunately, you won't have to fight for an inexpensive lunch at the Commerce Department cafeteria on the same floor. The aquarium is open from 9:00 A.M. to 5:00 P.M. daily; 482–2825 (information tape) or

The House Where Lincoln Died

*A*lthough Ford's Theater is clearly on the beaten path, surprisingly few of its visitors wander across the street to the modest rooming house where the mortally wounded Abraham Lincoln was carried up the curved stairs and died several hours later.

At the **Petersen House,** 516 Tenth Street NW, you enter through the front parlor where Mary Lincoln kept her anguished deathwatch. Like the rest of the house, the parlor is furnished in the style of an 1865 boardinghouse. The wall clock is stopped forever at 7:22 A.M., the precise moment of Lincoln's death. The adjoining room, where Secretary of War Edwin Stanton chaired cabinet meetings and arranged the orderly transfer of presidential power, became the de facto seat of government as Lincoln lay dying next door.

Although Washington is full of imposing sites connected with historic events, the Petersen House's modest bedroom is a sharp reminder that great history often appears unstaged and in prosaic places. This humdrum, shabby room is dominated by the bed where the president died; next to it stands a dresser with a few period knickknacks. The Petersen House is open daily 9:00 a.m. to 5:00 p.m. Call 426–6924 or visit www.nps.gov/foth. Metro: Metro Center (red, orange, and blue lines).

482–2826 (live person), fax 482–4946. Admission is charged. Metro: Federal Triangle (orange and blue lines).

There's no way you're going to overlook the ***Old Post Office Pavilion*** on Pennsylvania Avenue between 11th and 12th Streets, another grand old building that narrowly escaped the wrecker's ball. When it was built in 1899 as headquarters for the Postmaster General and the Post Office Department, this twelve-story fortress of steel and granite was Washington's first "skyscraper," but the Post Office, known to its detractors as "The Old Tooth," fell into disfavor in later years because its massive design overwhelmed that of other buildings in the Federal Triangle area. This Victorian veteran was saved and rebuilt in 1977, and lives on as a combination of government offices and tourist attraction.

Although the building's multistory atrium draws many visitors for its architecture, busy food court, and tourist-oriented shops, the main attraction is the ride up the 315-foot clock tower to the observation deck, where National Park Service Rangers will show you around and explain the building's history. If you go, expect a terrific view out over the capital and its suburbs and, on a clear day, even as far as Virginia's Blue Ridge Mountains. While up there you'll also see the Congress Bells, a bicentennial gift from Britain, which replicate the bells in London's Westminster

Abbey. The Pavilion (606–8691) is open from 8:00 A.M. to 10:45 P.M. from mid-April to Labor Day; the rest of the year it's 10:00 A.M. to 5:45 P.M. Individual shops may keep different hours. The Web site for the pavilion is www.oldpostofficedc.com and for the tower, www.nps.gov/opot/index. htm. Metro: Federal Triangle (orange and blue lines).

If the words **National Geographic Society** conjure up images of grandma's attic and stacks of dusty magazines with yellow borders, a visit to Society headquarters at 1145 17th Street NW will help bring you up to date fast In Explorer's Hall, which rings the building's entrance lobby, interactive educational games and exhibits on the earth sciences, geography, and anthropology are presented. Space science is dramatized in *Earth Station One,* with its huge freestanding globe and a seventy-two-seat theater that simulates an orbital flight from 23,000 feet up; there are several showings every hour. The display area at the other end of Explorer's Hall regularly presents special exhibits of great explorations or destinations.

Nothing demonstrates the "new" National Geographic as much as its bright, colorful store, which sells the Society's excellent travel guides and videos, plus the great photos and maps everyone expects from the National Geographic. If you want to become an intrepid National Geographic Explorer, even if you're just hiking to school, buy yourself an official knapsack or tote. Open Monday through Saturday 9:00 A.M. to 5:00 P.M., Sunday 10:00 A.M. to 5:00 P.M., holidays 9:00 A.M. to 5:00 P.M. Call 857–7588.

The Society also sponsors a little-publicized lecture and film series, often about adventure travel, in the **Grosvenor Auditorium** around the corner at 1600 M Street NW. Tickets, which range from $4.00 to 15.00 per event, can get scarce, so check the schedule and buy in advance by calling 857–7700 (fax 857–7747). The Grosvenor's box office is open 9:00 A.M. to 5:00 P.M. Monday through Friday. Metro: Farragut North (red line) and Farragut West (orange line). Tickets, along with other information about the National Geographic, are also available at www.nationalgeographic.com.

Across M Street from the National Geographic is the Sumner School, named after Senator Charles Sumner, who was caned on the floor of the Senate after giving a speech against slavery. The school played a historic and crucial role in the education of black students in the District ever since it opened in 1873 as the city's first high school for blacks. In 1979 this classic redbrick schoolhouse became the **Sumner School Museum and Archives,** dedicated to fostering African-American culture, history, and accomplishment. Exhibits of art and history predominate, but you

Off The Beaten Path

Booklover's Delight

*T*here's not a dot-com in sight at **Chapters Literary Bookstore,** 1512 K Street NW, one of my favorite Washington bookstores, on or off the beaten path. As its name implies, this is a place for book lovers, with a large selection of fiction and literary biography, along with a good variety of poetry and travel. Check with the friendly, well-informed staff about Chapters' extensive program of readings and signings. Open Monday through Friday 9:30 A.M. to 6:30 P.M., Saturday 11:00 A.M. to 5:00 P.M. Phone 347–5495. Metro stop: McPherson Square (orange and blue lines).

also might find displays of textiles from Nigeria, paintings by black artists, or historic photographs of African-American life in bygone times. Charles Sumner School Museum, 1201 17th Street NW (442–6060, fax 442–6050) is open Monday through Saturday from 10:00 A.M. to 5:00 P.M. Metro: Farragut North (red line) and Farragut West (orange line).

Chess buffs should make a series of lightning moves to the **U.S. Chess Center** at 1501 M Street NW, where they'll find one of America's few chess museums. The center's exhibits contain scorebooks of great matches, chess trophies, and art, along with a vast assortment of chess memorabilia. On the walls, photographs and other mementos make up the Chess Hall of Fame, a series of displays honoring American chess champions, and in the center's gift shop, enthusiasts can pick up chess books, boards and sets, and even chess-themed T-shirts. The center emphasizes its instructional programs for children, in which about 2,000 local schoolkids are enrolled. The center also sponsors tournaments and evening games, but I'm told that walk-ins are only rarely able to find a pickup game. The center is open Monday through Friday nights, starting at 6:00 P.M. and on weekends from noon to 6:00 P.M. Call 857–4922 or visit www.chessctr.org. Metro: McPherson Square (orange and blue lines).

The **B'nai B'rith National Jewish Museum** covers the totality of the Jewish experience from antiquity down to the present. The Museum's rare and beautiful displays of Judaica include the 1790 correspondence between George Washington and the sexton of the first American synagogue in Newport, Rhode Island, as well as sixteenth-century European torahs and collections of historic ritual objects. Other exhibits trace Jewish history, explain dietary laws, and illustrate Jewish holidays and traditions. There's even "Stars of David," the Jewish American Sports Hall of Fame, a collection of sports memorabilia honoring athletes such as Sandy Koufax, Hank Greenberg, and Mark Spitz. In addition to these exhibitions from its permanent collection, the museum often hosts special shows of Jewish culture, art, and history. The B'nai B'rith National Jewish Museum and its lively museum store are located in the B'nai B'rith building at 1640 Rhode Island Avenue NW. Open Sunday through Friday 10:00 A.M. to 5:00 P.M., except during winter, when it closes at 3:30 P.M. Closed Saturdays and on Jewish holidays. Admission by contribution. Call 857–6583 or visit www.bnaibrith.org on-line. Metro: Farragut North (red line) and Farragut West (orange line).

PLACES TO STAY IN DOWNTOWN

The Governor's House, 1615 Rhode Island Avenue NW; 296–2100 or (800) 821–4367, fax 463–6614; www.governorshousewdc.com. A distinctive, recently renovated boutique hotel with spacious, well-furnished rooms. Located downtown near the National Geographic, but only 4 blocks from Dupont Circle. There's also a fitness center and large outdoor pool for escaping those Washington summers. Moderate. Metro: Dupont Circle or Farragut North (both on red line).

Hotel Harrington, 436 11th Street NW; 628–8140 or (800) 424–8532; www.hotelharrington.com. This family-owned, frill-free hostelry is a Washington institution and a perennial favorite of budget travelers and tour groups. The main reasons are its value and great location, where downtown Washington meets Pennsylvania Avenue and only a short walk from the National Mall. A cafeteria, coin laundry, and pub round out the package. Inexpensive. Metro: Metro Center (red, orange, and blue lines).

Hotel Mayflower, 1127 Connecticut Avenue NW; 347–3000; www.renaissancehotels.com/wassh. This National Historic Landmark opened in 1925 with Calvin Coolidge's inaugural ball, and it's been attracting the important and powerful ever since. FDR and Eleanor stayed here while waiting for the Hoovers to move out of 1600 Pennsylvania; Charles De Gaulle and Nikita Khrushchev also signed the register. With its majestic main promenade, top restaurants, and luxurious rooms, it's easy to see why. Molto expensive. Metro: Farragut North (red line).

Hotel Washington, 15th Street and Pennsylvania Avenue NW; 638–5900. Talk about a great location! This first-rate Italian Renaissance hotel built in 1918 overlooks the Washington Monument and the Treasury; many rooms have great views down Pennsylvania Avenue to the Capitol dome. From May to October you can dine in the rooftop Sky Room or have cocktails outside on the Sky Terrace and take in a view you'll never forget. But if you don't reserve in advance, it won't happen. Expensive. Metro: Metro Center (red, orange, and blue lines).

J. W. Marriott, 1331 Pennsylvania Avenue NW; 393–2000. Large (773 rooms) and a major meeting/convention place, this is the flagship of the Marriott chain. The J. W. Marriott is located at the crosshairs of downtown Washington, convenient to everything in the city center, including the White House, National Theater, and Lafayette Square. The hotel sits on top of National Place, a large shopping center with an assortment of stores and restaurants.

Expensive. Metro: Metro Center (red, orange, and blue lines).

PLACES TO EAT IN DOWNTOWN

Cosi Sandwich Bar, 1700 Pennsylvania Avenue NW; 638–7101. If you haven't been invited to lunch at 1600 Pennsylvania, don't despair. At Cosi you'll see oodles of White House staff dining decisively on tailor-made sandwiches of tandoori chicken or tuna salad and brie, or you can watch the President's men and women lining up boldly to carry out grilled vegetables and tasty salads. This branch of a successful New York chain has caught on in a big way in D.C., mainly because of its encyclopedic range of sandwich ingredients and its patented focaccia-style bread. Great for lunch after touring the Lafayette Square/White House neighborhood. No reservations. Inexpensive. Open Monday through Thursday 7:00 A.M. to 6:00 P.M., Friday 7:00 A.M. to 5:00 P.M., Saturday 9:00 A.M. to 6:00 P.M., and Sunday 9:00 A.M. to 5:00 P.M. Metro: Farragut West (blue and orange lines).

Loeb's, 15th and I Streets; 371–1150. If Kosher food

had a Mecca, this would be it. This storefront deli is for homesick New Yorkers or anyone else who likes thick sandwiches of corned beef, pastrami, or tongue. Cream soda and bagels too—so what's not to like? Just around the corner from Lafayette Square. Open 6:00 A.M. to 4:30 P.M. Monday through Friday. No reservations. Inexpensive. Metro: McPherson Square (orange and blue lines).

M&S Grill, 600 13th Street NW; 347–1500. The atmosphere is late Victorian mansion, with Tiffany glass ceilings, chandeliers, and polished walnut paneled walls. J. P. Morgan would feel right at home. M&S's American bistro menu

includes steaks, chops, and well-prepared fish and scampi, which is understandable in a restaurant owned by Seattle's McCormick and Schmick (M&S—get it?). Inventive salads and sides too. The wine list is good and well priced, but could be a tad longer. All this plus friendly, professional service. Open Monday 11:30 A.M. to 4:00 P.M., Tuesday through Friday 11:30 A.M. to 10:00 P.M., Saturday 4:00 to 11:00 P.M., Sunday 4:00 to 10:00 P.M. The lively bar is open until 11:00 P.M. Sunday and Monday, until 1:00 A.M. Tuesday through Saturday. Moderate. Metro stop: Metro Center (red, orange, and blue lines).

Where to Find the Author's Favorite Places to Eat in Downtown

The Palm 1225
19th Street NW; 293–9091
(see page 9 for full listing)

Maloney and Porcelli
601 Indiana Avenue NW; 478–8300
(see page 9 for full listing)

Smith and Wollensky
1112 19th Street NW; 446–1100
(see page 9 for full listing)

Bobby Van's Steakhouse
809 15th Street NW; 589–0060
(see page 9 for full listing)

Palomino
Reagan Building, corner of 13th Street and Pennsylvania Avenue NW; 842–09800
(see page 11 for full listing)

Red Sage, 605 14th Street NW; 638-4444. This dazzling Southwestern favorite is actually two restaurants in one. The always busy street-level bar and dining area is lively and informal, with a chili bar, lighter fare, and moderate prices; in the grill room downstairs the action is more serious (and expensive) with dishes such as chorizos and black bean terrine or chipotle shrimp on a buttermilk corncake. No reservations upstairs, but essential for downstairs dining. Upstairs hours: Monday through Saturday 11:45 A.M. to 11:45 P.M., Sunday 4:30 to 11:00 P.M. Grill hours: Monday through Friday 11:30 A.M. to 2:00 P.M., Saturday and Sunday 5:00 to 10:30 P.M. Moderate upstairs; expensive downstairs. If you liked Red Sage and want to take it home with you, go next door to the Red Sage Bakery and Store, practically incandescent with all those spices, hot sauces, and dried peppers. Open Monday through Friday 8:00 A.M. to 3:00 P.M. Metro: Metro Center (red, orange, and blue lines).

17th Street Bar and Grill, 1615 Rhode Island Avenue NW (in the Governor's House Hotel); 296-2100. This attractive bistro with friendly service is well located for downtown lunches and dinners. American bistro also describes the food, which ranges from sandwiches, large salads, and pizza to grilled fish and steaks. Outside patio is open in good weather. Reserve, especially for lunch, when the National Geographic folks get out their maps and head this way. Moderate. Open Monday through Friday 7:00 A.M. to 10:00 P.M., Saturday 6:30 to 11 P.M., and Sunday 5:00 to 10:00 P.M. Metro: Farragut North (red line) and Farragut West (orange line).

The Old Ebbitt Grill, 675 15th Street NW; 347-4801. Located across from Treasury this is a big local favorite with a long history, where the decor is early McKinley and the food is refined American bistro. Favorites include steaks, grilled fish of all kinds, great crab cakes, and fresh oysters from all over. The liver and onions will make you forget mom's forced feeding; the burgers are classics. The Ebbitt's two immense bars are always crowded. First-rate Sunday brunch. Very popular with politicos, real Washingtonians and visitors, making reservations a must. Moderate. Open Monday through Friday 7:30 A.M. to 2:00 A.M., Saturday 8:30 A.M. to 2:00 A.M., Sunday 9:30 A.M. to 2:00 A.M. Metro: Metro Center (red, orange, and blue lines).

Tuscana West, 1350 I Street NW; 289-7300. This downtown Italian is a favorite of the lawyers, lobbyists, and other denizens of nearby K Street's "glitter gulch." Despite its name, Tuscana West offers dishes from all over Italy, including hearty northern risottos and southern pastas with heavy-duty red sauce, along with Tuscany's famed veal chops and seafood. Reservations advised. Moderate. Open Monday through Friday 10:30 A.M. to 10:30 P.M., Saturday 5:30 P.M. to midnight; closed Sunday. Metro: McPherson Square (blue and orange lines).

Pennsylvania Quarter and Chinatown

'Enfant's original plan for Washington envisioned the area around Seventh Street and Pennsylvania Avenue as the hub of the capital's civic life, where the courts, main government buildings, and city hall would be located. And they were. Washington's courthouse and judicial complex, along with great neoclassic public buildings, like the Patent Office and the now abandoned Old Post Office at Seventh and E Streets were built in this neighborhood and are still there. In later years, the Seventh Street area also became the place to shop for produce at the mammoth Center Market on Pennsylvania Avenue, which operated from 1801 to 1931 on the site of today's National Archives. Seventh Street also became the heart of the city's dry goods district, where Mr. Saks built his first store before moving on to Fifth Avenue. Local department stores like Hecht's, Kann's, and Woodward and Lothrop dominated the area until the 1960s, when the Seventh Street neighborhood fell into disrepair.

The late 1980s saw the Seventh Street corridor, now known as the "New Downtown" or "Pennsylvania Quarter," stage a rebound that's still in progress, thanks in part to the construction of the MCI sports complex and the arrival of trendy art galleries and restaurants. Today the revitalized Seventh Street corridor boasts an intense gallery and art scene, some of the city's most innovative restaurants, a world-class Shakespearean theater, and a pair of unforgettable museums. It is also the gateway to Washington's Chinatown.

Two Metro stops serve the Pennsylvania Quarter: at the Chinatown end through the Gallery Place/Chinatown stop on the yellow, red, and green lines and at the Pennsylvania Avenue end through the Archives/Navy Memorial stop on the yellow and green lines.

Start your visit to the Pennsylvania Quarter at the *Navy Memorial,* which proves that even well-beaten paths like Pennsylvania Avenue can have hidden corners. This impressive but simple memorial—with its

Pennsylvania Quarter and Chinatown

PENNSYLVANIA QUARTER AND CHINATOWN

TOP ATTRACTIONS IN THE
PENNSYLVANIA QUARTER AND CHINATOWN

*National Museum of
American Art*

National Portrait Gallery

The Naval Heritage Center

406 Seventh Street

Footnotes Cafe

Shakespeare Theater

Old Pension Building

National Building Museum

The Wilson Center Gallery

Corso dei Fiori

Cafe Atlantico

MCI Center

Chinatown

The National Law Enforcement Officers Memorial

Morrison-Clark Inn

fountains, ship's masts with signal flags, and the touching statue of the *Lone Sailor*—commemorates the Navy's battles, heroism, and achievements. Two curved sculpture walls record important Navy accomplishments and scenes from Navy history. With any luck at all, you'll be there for one of the frequent outdoor concerts by the Navy Band or a visiting musical group.

But less well known, even to many Washingtonians, is the privately funded *Naval Heritage Center.* The center's entrance hall adjoins the Memorial on street level, but the real action is below deck, on an underground floor where exhibits depict Navy traditions and a "Ship's Store" sells nautical mementos, prints, and books. The center also has a state-of-the-art theater showing *At Sea,* an action-packed film about carrier life. And don't miss "Navy Log," where you can search military records on a 250,000-name computerized database to see if your Navy or Marine pals haven't been exaggerating their war stories.

The Naval Heritage Center, at 701 Pennsylvania Avenue NW (737–2300), is open Monday through Saturday 9:30 A.M. to 5:00 P.M.; closed Sunday. From November to February the center is also closed Mondays. E-mail ahoy@lonesailor.org or visit www.lonesailor.org. Metro: Archives/Navy Memorial (green and yellow lines).

Just off Seventh Street on Indiana Avenue stand a trio of well-preserved 1820 houses that knew Lincoln, when the President's carriage took him up Seventh Street to his summer White House at the Soldier's Home. Fine residential dwellings in their day, these antebellum homes have long since been converted to commercial use. The house at 641 Indiana is where you'll find *Artifactory,* a large collection of art and handicrafts unearthed by owner Dominick Cardella on his travels in Africa and Asia. Cardella's shop is packed with an eclectic and tasteful selection of artifacts that includes marionettes from Burma and Indonesia, Balinese masks, and traditional African art and statuary. Artifactory is open Monday through Saturday 10:00 A.M. to 6:00 P.M. Call 393–2727. Metro: Archives/Navy Memorial (yellow and green lines).

The top three floors of 406 Seventh Street are entirely given over to several of Washington's top galleries, where a range of artists, from New

OFF THE BEATEN PATH

> ### America's Oldest Otis Elevator
>
> *The 1852 vintage rope-powered lift in Litwin's Furniture and Antiques at 637 Indiana Avenue is the oldest known Otis elevator in America, and it's still in use.*

York's best painters and photographers to Washington's own up-and-coming talent, exhibit in spare, high-ceilinged rooms perfect for showing off their colorful art and photography. In addition to their regular hours, all of the galleries are open from 6:00 to 8:00 P.M. on the third Thursday of every month.

The third-floor **Numark Gallery** features New York artists such as David Row, David Shapiro, and minimalist Sol Lewitt, along with Washingtonians like Robin Rose and Christopher French. Numark Gallery (628–3810, www.numarkgallery.com) is open Tuesday through Saturday 11:00 A.M. to 6:00 P.M. Next door, the **David Adamson Gallery** focuses on digital printmaking and photography, but also offers prints and paintings by New York and local artists. Open Tuesday through Saturday 11:00 A.M. to 5:30 P.M. Call 628–0257 or visit www.adamsoneditions. com. The **Washington Center for Photography** (737–0406), a community arts center open Wednesday through Saturday from noon to 5:00 P.M., showcases the work of local and national photographers; the center also sponsors workshops and lecture programs.

In the sprawling second-floor **Artist's Museum,** there's enough space for up to five artists to stage their own shows simultaneously. During one of my visits I got a world tour of art and artists from Washington, France, New York, and the Czech Republic, including an inspired and slightly wacky model by Museum Director David Stainback of a windowed Washington Monument converted to a condominium. Artist's Museum is open Tuesday through Saturday 11:00 A.M. to 6:00 P.M. Call 638–7001 or e-mail: amuseum@erols.com. Visitors to 406 Seventh Street can also browse and buy a variety of media, including abstract paintings, sculpture, and installation art at **Touchstone Gallery,** a cooperative gallery on the second floor. Open Wednesday through Friday 11:00 A.M. to 5:00 P.M., Saturday and Sunday noon to 5:00 P.M. Call 347–2787.

Even the storefront at 406 offers art, but of a slightly different kind. At **Apartment Zero** you'll find one of D.C.'s hippest home furnishings stores, with cutting-edge office and home furniture, standing lamps of sculptured paper, and, in season, unique Christmas tree ornaments. Nick and Nora Charles would really go for Apartment Zero's collection of '30s era martini shakers, glassware, and other cocktail paraphernalia, minus the olives. Shop here and your house will never be the same Open Tuesday through Saturday 11:00 A.M. to 8:00 P.M., Sunday noon to 5:00 P.M. Call 628–4067 or visit www.apartmentzero.com. Metro: Archives/Navy Memorial (yellow and green lines).

PENNSYLVANIA QUARTER AND CHINATOWN

AUTHOR'S FAVORITES IN THE
PENNSYLVANIA QUARTER AND CHINATOWN

Old Pension Building

Jaleo

MCI National Sports Gallery

Teaism

Temperance Fountain

Although there's a Starbucks in the next block, *Footnotes Cafe* seems to be the coffeehouse of choice for Penn Quarter gallery goers and book browsers. Located in the Seventh Street branch of Olsson's, an outstanding local chain of book and record sellers, Footnotes has a wide range of coffees and teas, a good but short wine list, and a selection of erudite sandwiches for literary noshing. Try ordering the Charles Dickens (traditional roast beef), the Herman Melville ("a whale of a tuna sandwich"), or, if the bambini are along, the Dr. Seuss, which (no surprise here) is peanut butter and jelly. Tables with chairs and sofas round out the picture and, should you feel like falling into a literary swoon, there's a cut velvet chaise longue available in the window. Footnotes, located at 418 Seventh Street, is open weekdays 8:00 A.M. to 7:30 P.M., Saturday 10:00 A.M. to 7:30 P.M., and Sunday noon to 7:30 P.M.; Afternoon tea from 3:00 to 6:00 P.M. Call 638–4882. Metro: Archives/Navy Memorial (yellow and green lines).

Pua, the shop at 444 Seventh Street NW, takes its name from a natural plant fiber produced in the Himalayas, then spun and woven by hand by Nepalese craftswomen. Pua's designs include quilted cotton coats and jackets, colorful and attractive dresses, and block printed skirts and pants. While you're deciding, have a cup of Darjeeling in Pua's little tearoom. Open Monday noon to 6:00 P.M., Tuesday through Friday noon to 7:30 P.M., Saturday and Sunday 1:00 to 7:30 P.M. Call 347–4543. Metro: Archives/Navy Memorial (yellow and green lines).

The first thing to notice about *The Mark,* at 401 Seventh Street, is its location, a once abandoned Victorian office building just like the classic nineteenth-century structures that line the streets of New York City's Cast Iron district. The second is the cool decor, with tiny purple drop lights, black marble-topped tables, and colorful wall art, all to the accompaniment of equally cool jazz. Don't let any of this distract you from chef Alison Swope's inventive cooking, which manager Phil Jacobsen describes as "robust New American." Signature dishes include lamb and dried cherry sausage, a miso-glazed Norwegian salmon, and ravioli with andouille and shrimp. The Mark also has a nice assortment of California varietals at reasonable prices. For lighter fare, go next door to The Mark's take-out sibling, known as, you guessed it, *The Markette,* where you'll find inventive sandwiches along with old standbys like grilled cheese or tuna salad, plus Chef Swope's "outrageous soups." The Mark is open Monday through Saturday for lunch from 11:30 A.M. to 3:00 P.M. and for dinner at 5:00 P.M.; closed Sundays. Reservations are

The Venerable Bead

*W*hoever said, "when you've seen one bead museum, you've seen 'em all" clearly had never cast a beady eye on Suite 202 at 400 Seventh Street NW. The **Washington Bead Museum's** spacious loft hosts a continuous round of exhibits of handmade glass beads, period glass, and jewelry from all over, most recently the United States, the Czech Republic, India, and Africa. Aside from attracting a worldwide audience of bead enthusiasts, the museum also sponsors a series of educational programs to illustrate how beadwork reflects a society's craftsmanship, traditions, and history. Open Monday, Wednesday, and Saturday 11:00 A.M. to 4:00 P.M., Sunday 1:00 to 4:00 P.M. Call 624–4500, visit www.thebead museum.org, or e-mail: beadmus@ erols.com.

advised. Call 783–3133 or visit www.mark-restaurant.com. Moderate. The Markette is open Monday through Friday 11:00 A.M. to 5:00 P.M. Inexpensive. Metro: Archives/Navy Memorial (yellow and green lines).

The *Zenith Gallery* is a Pennsylvania Quarter pioneer, having arrived at 413 Seventh Street in 1986. It is also one of the neighborhood's more eclectic galleries, where you'll find sculptures in bronze, steel, wood, and ceramic, abstract and realistic paintings, and other media ranging from light sculptures to wearable art, furniture, and comical figures of papier-mâché and resin. After checking out the street-level space, head for the downstairs gallery to see more of Zenith's original and witty offerings. As a bonus, along the way you'll pass through the architectural gem at 409 Seventh Street. Built in 1979, it replaced a structure that connected the two vintage Victorian office buildings on either side. If you have a taste for whimsy, the Zenith is for you. The Zenith Gallery is open Monday 11 A.M. to 4 P.M., Tuesday through Friday 11 A.M. to 6 P.M., Saturday noon to 7:00 P.M., and Sunday noon to 5:00 P.M. Closed Mondays in January. Call 783–2963, fax 783-0050, e-mail: zenithga@erols.com or visit www.zenithgallery.com. Metro: Archives/Navy Memorial (yellow and green lines).

Tucked away behind the modest marquee at 450 Seventh Street is the 441-seat *Shakespeare Theater,* which *The Economist* called "one of the world's three great Shakespearean theatres," and the *Wall Street Journal* dubbed "the nation's foremost Shakespeare company." Since the Shakespeare opened in 1986, its performances have racked up dozens of awards, plus acclaim from the *New York Times* as a "critical and popular success." Outstanding guest actors such as Elizabeth Ashley,

PENNSYLVANIA QUARTER AND CHINATOWN

Chinese New Year

If you're in town during early February, call 638–1041 to learn the date and other details about Washington's annual Chinese New Year celebration, which is great fun, with enough fireworks to destroy a small country and a parade led by a giant dragon.

Hal Holbrook, and Patrick Stewart often join the resident company in staging Shakespearean and other classical plays during the theater's September to July season. Call 547–1122 for information on what's playing, to book seats, or to ask about the Shakespeare's outdoor summer performances in Rock Creek Park. The box office is open Monday 10:00 A.M. to 6:00 P.M., Tuesday through Saturday 10:00 A.M. to 7:30 P.M., and Sunday noon to 7:30 P.M. Metro: Archives/Navy Memorial (yellow and green lines).

Those walls covered with colorful plates and a giant mural of a flamenco dancer announce that you've arrived at *Jaleo,* a lively storefront Spanish bistro on the corner of Seventh and E Streets. If you're headed for the Shakespeare Theatre next door or the MCI Center up the street, this bright and bustling restaurant with friendly service is perfect for a pre- or postperformance snack or meal. Choose four or five hot or cold tapas, maybe some garlic shrimp, grilled lamb, or peppers stuffed with goat cheese, and you're off and running. But for a lot of people (like me), that's just the beginning, so they move on to Chef Jose Andres's excellent paellas, grilled fish, or fish stew. Grilled spicy Spanish chorizos (sausages), either as tapas or as a main dish with beans and asparagus, are always a good choice. And, no surprise, the gazpacho and sangria are terrific. As in Madrid, the dinner and bar action goes on until late, when a trendy younger crowd takes over and Jaleo begins to live up to its name—which translates as uproar or revelry—especially on Wednesday nights, when the dancers from Seville perform. Bring castanets. Jaleo, 480 Seventh Street NW (628–7949), is open Sunday and Monday 11:30 A.M. to 10:00 P.M., Tuesday through Thursday 11:30 A.M. to 11:30 P.M., Friday and Saturday 11:30 A.M. to midnight. Although Jaleo accepts a limited number of preshow reservations from 5:00 to 6:30 P.M., seating at other times is walk-in. Moderate. Metro: Archives/Navy Memorial (yellow and green lines).

That massive Greek Revival building on Seventh between F and G Streets is the **Old Patent Office,** which dates from the 1830s, when old photos show its elegant columns beginning to rise above the swamplands and meadows of a distinctly rustic Washington. During the Civil War the Patent Office became a Union Army barracks and hospital where two government clerks, poet Walt Whitman and American Red Cross founder Clara Barton, served as volunteer nurses. Lincoln's second inaugural ball was held in the vast, marble-columned room on the

National Portrait Gallery, Old Patent Office

third floor known today as the Lincoln Gallery. The building's Victorian gingerbread Great Hall was once the largest room in America and is still one of the most ornate and beautiful.

Since 1968 this Washington landmark has housed two of the capital's finest museums: the National Portrait Gallery, with stunning portraits of the men and women who shaped American history, from George Washington to Ernest Hemingway, and the National Museum of American Art, dedicated to the entire span of American artistic creativity. Alas, you won't be able to wander the antebellum corridors to enjoy these two museums until sometime in 2003, when the building reopens after an extensive renovation. But on the internet you can get a good idea of what you'll see when they reopen. The National Museum of American Art address is www.nmaa.si.edu, while many of the National Portrait Gallery's treasures can be found at www.npg.si.edu.

You can't miss the ***Old Pension Building,*** the spectacular redbrick Victorian pile on F Street that occupies the entire block between Fourth and Fifth Streets. The building, inspired by Rome's Palazzo Farnese, is circled by a terra-cotta frieze of the Union Army and Navy in action, complete with bayonet charges, sea battles, and gallant generals on rearing chargers, your clue that the building was constructed to process Civil War veterans' benefits. But this is far from being a maze of cubicles for Civil Service paper pushers. You'll be astounded by the grandeur of the Pension Building's Great Hall, a 300-foot-long interior courtyard supported by eight colossal marble columns with a fountain in the center. It's the perfect place for a large and elegant party, which is exactly why presidents since Grover Cleveland have been using the Great Hall for their inaugural balls.

The magnificent setting tends to overshadow the *National Building Museum,* which now occupies part of this grand space. The museum, which celebrates the building arts, nevertheless holds its own with a series of lively exhibits ranging from the American country store to the impact of air-conditioning on everyday life. Don't miss the permanent exhibit *Washington: Symbol and City,* an excellent orientation to the history of the Federal City, the evolution of its architecture, and the impact of European cities on Washington's urban plan. The museum shop is well-stocked with books on buildings and architecture; in Blueprints Cafe you'll find coffee, salads, and a selection of sandwiches named for noted architects. The "Mies Van der Rohe" combines form and function to come up with peanut butter and jelly. The Building Museum (272–2448, www.nbm.org) is at 401 F Street NW. From June through August, museum hours are Monday through Saturday 10 A.M. to 5 P.M., Sunday noon to 5:00 P.M. The rest of the year it is open Monday through Saturday 10 A.M. to 4 P.M., and Sunday noon to 4:00 P.M. Building tours, which last forty-five minutes, are given Monday through Wednesday at 12:30 P.M., Thursday through Saturday at 11:30 A.M., 12:30 and 1:30 P.M., and Sunday at 12:30 and 1:30 P.M. Reservations are not needed and there is no charge. Metro: Judiciary Square (red line).

The District's *Recorder of Deeds Building* at 515 D Street NW may not amount to much aesthetically, but it contains a set of wonderful murals

Honoring the Men in Blue

*T*he *National Law Enforcement Officers Memorial,* across F Street from the National Building Museum, bears the names of the 14,500 American law enforcement officers killed in the line of duty since 1794. Like the Vietnam Memorial, the wall of inscriptions is frequently visited by relatives or colleagues of the fallen officers, who often leave flowers in remembrance. Although the memorial reminds visitors that violence is always just around the corner for law enforcers, it is also a restful, nicely landscaped place to stroll or take a break from gallery- and museum-hopping.

The *National Law Enforcement Visitors Center,* a short walk away at 605 E Street, is the Memorial's companion, a collection of exhibits honoring officers killed in the line of duty. There is also a display of legendary policemen, whose ranks include New York Police Commissioner Teddy Roosevelt, "Untouchable" Eliot Ness, and Wild West lawman Wyatt Earp. The Visitors Center is open Monday through Friday 9 A.M. to 5:00 P.M., Saturday 10:00 A.M. to 5:00 P.M., and Sunday noon to 5:00 P.M. Call 737–3400, visit www.nleomf.com, or e-mail lisaletke@erols.com.

Urban Preservation

*T*he **Morrison-Clark Inn** *is a prime example of how urban preservation and restoration can enrich the lives of Washington's residents and visitors. This grand Victorian mansion at Massachusetts Avenue and 11th Street actually represents the twentieth-century merger of a pair of handsome homes built in 1864 by wealthy merchants David Morrison and Reuben Clark. A subsequent owner of the Morrison house (obviously a Sinophile) added the grand Chinese Chippendale porch and graceful Shanghai roof visible on the Massachusetts Avenue side of the inn. Through fifty-seven years and two World Wars, the house served as an inexpensive residence and club for enlisted men until 1987, when it was extensively renovated and opened as the elegant hotel and restaurant that it is today.*

As men of wealth and taste, Messrs. Morrison and Clark would feel right at home in this upscale urban inn. Floor-to-ceiling pier mirrors face each other across a lobby with antebellum furniture and a marble fireplace. The Victorian feel is reflected in the upstairs guest rooms, with their massive armoires, antique furnishings, and imposing mahogany headboards. If you go, ask about room 215, with its private entrance to the porch and a great view up and down Massachusetts Avenue. The inn also offers its guests several French country–style rooms and parlor suites with wicker furniture and pine armoires.

The inn is home to one of Washington's top restaurants, where Chef Bob Beaudry, despite his New England origins, specializes in imaginative American cuisine with a definite southern accent. That explains why your first course might be grits soufflé, chili-seasoned chicken fingers, or a salad of roasted baby beets. Entrees include spice-seared salmon or tuna, and at lunch a robust beef potpie or a saffron and leek "pizza." Morrison-Clark signature dishes include two perennials, the romaine-Roquefort salad with walnut focaccia and the exquisite lemon chess pie. All of this culinary delight takes place in an elegant Victorian dining room with tall windows, more full-length gilded mirrors and drapes, and a central banquette of unobtrusive chinoiserie. It is regularly named as one of Washington's most romantic restaurants.

The Morrison-Clark Inn (www. morrisonclark.com) is located at 1015 L Street NW in the Penn Quarter. Call 898–1200 or (800) 332–7898; fax 289–8576. The dining room is open Monday through Friday 11:00 A.M. to 2 P.M. and 6:00 to 9:30 P.M., Saturday 6:00 to 10:00 P.M., Sunday brunch 11:00 A.M. to 2:00 P.M. and dinner 6:00 to 9:00 P.M. The inn and its restaurant are both expensive. Metro: Mt. Vernon. Square (yellow and green lines).

representing important leaders and events throughout African-American history. The series begins in the entrance hall by honoring scientist Benjamin Banneker; six others depict Frederick Douglass in his role as

adviser to Abraham Lincoln, Col. Robert Shaw and the 54th Massachusetts at the siege of Confederate Fort Wagner, and explorer Matthew
Henson at the South Pole with Admiral Peary. These imposing paintings, like many in post offices and other public buildings throughout
the United States, were commissioned by the Public Works Administration, which means that they date from the early 1940s. The building is
open Monday through Friday from 8:30 A.M. to 4:00 P.M. Metro:
Archives/Navy Memorial (yellow and green lines).

Before you enter *Miya,* at 629 E Street NW, look over the door at the
wild mosaic facade with a giant phoenix, glittery swirls, and a man
about to take a header onto E Street. Inside, Miya is crammed with
African-American art and artifacts, including lots of weavings, mats,
and tapestries. Open Monday through Friday noon to 7:00 P.M., Saturday 1:00 to 5:00 P.M.; closed Sunday. Call 347–6330.

Be sure to visit the *Wilson Center Gallery,* a nonprofit cooperative run
by its 125 artist-members, which provides affordable studio, exhibition,
and teaching space for local artists. It's also where visitors can buy their
work or chat up the artist who's minding the gallery at the time. The
Wilson Center sponsors a number of shows each year, including a
December "Holiday Artisan Show" that's a perfect occasion to pick up
special gift items, including wheel-thrown pottery, exotic woven shawls
or scarves, and an assortment of jewelry. Wilson Center Gallery, 501 E
Street NW is open Tuesday through Saturday 11:00 A.M. to 6:00 P.M., and
Sunday 11:00 A.M. to 4:00 P.M. Call 882–0740.

When my wife and I lived in Rome, our idea of a great time was to drive
up to the Umbrian ceramics mecca of Deruta, where we'd look at hand-
painted tiles and pottery and dream about the Italian country home we
never quite bought. If you'd like to do some dreaming of your own, leave
your passport in the drawer and head for *Corso dei Fiori* at Eighth and D
Streets. In fact, Deruta is exactly where Corso dei Fiori has its own workshops, so if you actually did buy that Italian dream home, or just love
great ceramics, check out Corso dei Fiori's colorful and remarkable collection of table settings, cachepots, and planters. And there's other classy
stuff for your Tuscan villa, including all of the old-shoe English and Italian furniture you'll ever need to spiff up your *sala di pranzo*. Dream on.
Open Monday through Friday 10:00 A.M. to 6:00 P.M., Saturday 11 A.M. to 4
P.M.; closed Sunday. Call 628–1929 or visit www.corso.com. Metro:
Archives/Navy Memorial (yellow and green lines).

At *Cafe Atlantico* the accent is on Latin America and its exciting *nueva
cocina*. Dining is on three dramatically staged levels, each displaying

Hooker's Army

*W*hen the Civil War brought hundreds of thousands of soldiers to Washington, something occurred that Pierre L'Enfant, the great planner, could never have foreseen. Pennsylvania Avenue, a.k.a. "America's Main Street," turned into America's leading red-light district, where hundreds of Washington hostesses gathered every evening around Seventh Street. Union General Joseph Hooker, concerned about this, ordered the ladies and their activities confined to a nearby neighborhood known today as Federal Triangle, a command that caused them to refer to themselves sarcastically as "Hooker's Army," and so the term "hooker" was born. Archaeological note: Excavations for major buildings in this area have turned up perfume and liquor bottles, combs, and garter hooks.

the work of South American and Caribbean artists. Thirsty gringos can belly up the bar for potent *bebidas latinas* like silky margaritas and tasty but lethal pisco sours. If a few of these Pan-American power-houses haven't sent you south of the border, order one of the restaurant's imaginative specialties such as Brazilian feijoada with an Asian spin, duck confit, or a plump grilled salmon wrapped in papaya. There's usually a tasting menu, and at Saturday lunch the main attraction is an inventive and popular Latin American dim sum platter. Reservations recommended; to get them, call 393–0812. Cafe Atlantico, at 405 Eighth Street NW, serves lunch 11:30 A.M. to 2:30 P.M. Monday through Thursday and dinner from 5:00 to10:00 P.M. On Friday and Saturday lunch hours are 11:30 A.M. to 1:30 P.M. and dinner is served from 5:00 to 11:00 P.M. Sunday it's dinner only, from 5:00 to 11:00 P.M. Expensive.

Across the street at 400 Eighth Street, in the bright, airy *Teaism* restaurant, you can dine in utter tranquility on everything from miso soup and soba noodle salad to *ochazuke,* which is Japanese rice and tea soup. Teaism also specializes in "big dishes" of curries and rice, but for a real change of pace, try a "bento" or Japanese meal box based on salmon, beef, or tuna. Teaism's eclectic menu also offers breakfasts of French toast, chicken sausage with naan and raita, and (need we say it?) a vast repertoire of teas and tisanes. Open Monday through Friday 7:30 A.M. to 10:30 P.M., Saturday and Sunday 9:30 A.M. to 11:30 P.M. Call 638–6010.

If you liked Teaism enough to take it home with you, pop into the restaurant's tea shop next door to pick up some Jasmine Pearl or Anxi for your very own, and carry it away in a gorgeous tea box made with colorful washi paper. Here you'll also find all the tea paraphernalia you could ever need, including all of the exotic sweets, jams, and chocolates needed to wow your pals with a great high tea. Open Monday through Friday 11:00 A.M. to 7:00 P.M., Saturday noon to 7:00 P.M., Sunday noon to 5:00 P.M. Call 638–7740.

The **MCI Center,** with its banners and imposing facade, has been the centerpiece of this neighborhood and of the Washington sports and cultural scene since the day it opened its doors in 1998. The Center hosts professional teams like the NBA Wizards, the WNBA Mystics, the NHL Capitals and the Georgetown University Hoyas, along with a variety of concerts. But even when there's no sporting or cultural event going on, the center offers a broad array of attractions.

One of the most popular is the **MCI National Sports Gallery,** on the center's third floor, which showcases American sports memorabilia, including Babe Ruth's bat, Muhammad Ali's robe and a Michael Jordan jersey. Fans with a rich fantasy life can also go *mano a mano* with the pros in interactive baseball and basketball matches or relive great moments in sports by video and radio. The museum is also home to the American Sportscasters Association Hall of Fame and Museum. Admission is $5.00, children five and under get in free. Open Tuesday through Sunday 11:00 A.M. to 6:00 P.M.; closed Mondays. Call 661–5133.

The center's **Discovery Channel Store** is a real kid magnet—a three-level, 25,000-square-foot museum shop with educational and entertaining displays, including a three-story dinosaur (major even by

MCI Center

31

dinosaur standards), a giant ant colony, and other scientific exhibits. The store also shows *Destination DC,* a fifteen-minute high-definition film that gives a first-rate overview of the Federal City. The store is open daily 10:00 A.M. to 10:00 P.M. Admission to *Destination DC* is $2.50 for adults, $1.50 for children and seniors.

The MCI Center, at 601 F Street NW, is open daily 10:00 A.M. to 10:00 P.M. (or one hour after Center events conclude), Sunday 10:00 A.M. to 6:00 P.M. For information, call 628–3200; for seats it's 432–7328, or go on-line at www.mcicenter.com. And on the way out, don't miss the photographic exhibit of neighborhood history just inside the F Street entrance. Metro: Gallery Place/Chinatown (red, yellow, and green lines).

If you're accustomed to visiting Chinatowns in San Francisco or New York, D.C.'s version is going to seem pretty puny, its main attraction being the ornate and colorful archway at Seventh and H Streets. Chinatown's Metro stop is, logically enough, Gallery Place/Chinatown on the red, yellow, and green lines.

Although it lacks the scale and variety of its counterparts elsewhere, Washington's **Chinatown** does offer a broad array of good and inexpensive Chinese restaurants. My favorite is **Hunan Chinatown** at 624 H Street (783–5858), where the fried dumplings and the smoked duck are memorable. If you want to combine dining with history, head for **Go-Lo's** at 604 H Street (347–4656), a modest but good restaurant located in the house of Mary Surratt, where the Lincoln assassination conspiracy was hatched. Mary was hanged for her role in the plot, but don't let that spoil your General Tso's chicken or shredded beef. Both restaurants are open daily for lunch and dinner.

Strange Monument to Sobriety

A few steps from the Navy Memorial, on Indiana Plaza at Seventh Street and Pennsylvania, stands the **Temperance Fountain,** *one of the weirdest statues in a city where bizarre statuary is as common as fund-raising. Note the intertwined fish under four granite pillars surmounted by a triumphant bronze heron (I am not making this up). This powerful inducement to sobriety was erected in the city's former good-time district by (wait, this gets even more bizarre) a California temperance crusader who made his fortune making false teeth. The fountain once spouted water to give thirsty passersby a big, free drink, but the spigot was turned off long ago and the fountain went dry. The city definitely did not.*

Then there's the "only in America" block, the 800 block of Seventh Street. Here, in the heart of Chinatown and surrounded by street and other signs in Chinese, you'll find lined up *(a)* an Irish pub and restaurant, *(b)* a Brazilian-Mexican restaurant, and *(c)* the German Cultural Institute, which presents rich programs of German film, music, and theater.

The Irish bar is **Fado,** which specializes in boxty (an Irish potato pancake stuffed with salmon or steak), shepherd's pie, and the inevitable corned beef and cabbage. Fado is located at 808 Seventh Street NW and is open Sunday through Thursday 11:30 A.M. to 2:00 A.M., Friday and Saturday 11:30 A.M. to 3:00 A.M. Call 789–0066. Inexpensive.

Coco Loco offers an eclectic mix of Brazilian and contemporary Mexican cuisine, including tapas, chiles rellenos, and, for real carnivores, an all-you-can-eat *churrascaria,* a culinary pageant of beef, pork, and chicken served at your table. The bar is home to the deadly *capirinha,* a Brazilian rum-lime combination and the dreaded *batida,* a high-octane mix of rum and coconut milk that, if it's not banned by an international agreement, should be. After 11:00 P.M. on Friday and Saturday, the restaurant turns into a nightclub where, after a few *batidas* anyone can samba with the best of them and pretend it's Carnival in Rio. Coco Loco, at 810 Seventh Street NW, serves food Monday through Saturday 11:30 A.M. to 2:30 P.M. and 5:30 P.M. to 11:30 P.M. Call 289–2626. Moderate.

The German Cultural Center, the **Goethe Institute,** sponsors a wide selection of art exhibits, lectures, and other cultural programs. And if you've always wanted to learn a little Deutsch, there are courses for that as well. The institute is located at 810 Seventh Street and is open Monday through Friday 9:00 A.M. to 5:00 P.M. Call 289–1200 for information about exhibits and cultural programs.

PLACES TO STAY IN THE PENNSYLVANIA QUARTER AND CHINATOWN

Henley Park Hotel, 926 Massachusetts Avenue NW; 638–5200 or (800) 222–8474. This Tudor-style building began life in 1918 as an apartment house, but it's now the urban equivalent of an English country inn. Its seventy-nine rooms and seventeen suites are mainly done in Chippendale, with four-poster beds, antiques, parquet floors, and overstuffed chairs. Cozy, well-mannered, and chintzy in the nice sense—Edith Wharton will be along any minute. The Henley's restaurant, Coeur de Lion, is, however, strictly non-British, specializing in New American fare; nice atrium too. Hotel and restaurant are both expensive.

Courtyard by Marriott, Ninth and F Streets NW; 638–4600. If, like Gordon Gekko in *Wall Street,* you think that "greed is good," and the idea of spending the night snuggled up with some cash has a certain appeal, then this is just the place for you. The Courtyard is located in an 1891 vintage bank that was clearly designed to impress depositors, with its massive stone facade, coffered ceilings, and marble staircases in the lobby. This classic example of urban conversion features a restaurant, the Courtyard Cafe (located among the safe deposit boxes), and a conference area in the former vault. The rooms are equally imposing. Moderate.

PLACES TO EAT IN
THE PENNSYLVANIA
QUARTER AND CHINATOWN

Luigino, 1100 New York Avenue; 371–0595, www.luigino.com. Every meal in this handsome, bustling restaurant brings back memories of my favorite ristorante in Milan. Signor Luigino serves up northern Italian favorites like risotto, sweetbreads, and game specialties, plus pastas made *in casa*, including my all-time favorite, pappardelle in hare sauce. Open for lunch 11:30 A.M. to 2:30 P.M. weekdays. Dinner is served Monday

through Thursday 5:30 to 10:30 P.M., Friday and Saturday 5:30 to 11:00 P.M., Sunday 5:00 to 10:00 P.M. Moderate.

Capital Grill, 601 Pennsylvania Avenue NW; 737–6200. The sides of beef hanging in the window say it all. This upscale steak house lures political moguls of both parties from Capitol Hill, probably because of the men's club atmosphere and lively bar scene. All this and terrific steaks and lobsters too. Testosterone levels positively soar in the special cigar areas. Reservations essential. Open Monday through Thursday 11:30 A.M. to 10:00 P.M., Friday until 11:00 P.M., Saturday 5:00 to 11:00 P.M., Sunday 5:00 to 10:00 P.M. Expensive.

Austin Grill, 750 E Street NW; 393–3776. You'll see why this Penn Quarter outpost of a local chain is so popular when you tuck into the quesadillas and fajitas, not to mention all those

silky margaritas. Standard Tex-Mex offerings in a relaxed atmosphere, probably because the decor is early Texas roadhouse. Open Monday through Thursday 11:30 A.M. to 10:00 P.M., Friday and Saturday until midnight, Sunday 11:00 A.M. to 10:00 P.M. No reservations. Inexpensive.

District Chop House, 509 Seventh Street; 347–3434. Just what its name says, this steak house with billiard tables, oceans of beer, and early twentieth-century kitsch is another good place to know about if you're headed for the MCI Center or the Shakespeare Theater. Contrived but fun. Open Monday 11:00 A.M. to 10 P.M., Tuesday through Friday 11:00 A.M. to 11:00 P.M., Saturday 4:00 to 11:00 P.M., Sunday 4:00 to 10:00 P.M. Inexpensive.

Tony Cheng's, 619 H Street; 842–8669. Actually two restaurants in one. Upstairs the specialty is dim sum

Where to Find the Author's Favorite Places to Stay in Pennsylvania Quarter and Chinatown

Morrison-Clark Inn
*1015 L Street NW; 898–1200 or (800) 332–7898
(see page 28 for full listing)*

and seafood, such as stir-fried grouper or shrimp with asparagus in black bean sauce. Downstairs try your hand at Mongolian barbecue or hot pot; the all-you-can-eat barbecue involves selecting the ingredients and giving them to the cooks for grilling, while the hot pot has you cooking your own vegetables and noodles in a pot of boiling stock. Open Sunday through Thursday 11:00 A.M. to 11:00 P.M., Friday and Saturday until midnight. Inexpensive.

Where to Find the Author's Favorite Places to Eat in Pennsylvania Quarter and Chinatown

Footnotes Cafe
418 Seventh Street; 638–4882
(see page 23 for full listing)

The Mark
401 Seventh Street; 783–3133
(see page 23 for full listing)

The Markette
Next door to The Mark
(see page 23 for full listing)

Morrison-Clark Inn
1015 L Street NW; 898–1200 or (800) 332–7898
(see page 28 for full listing)

Cafe Atlantico
405 Eighth Street NW; 393–0812
(see page 29 for full listing)

Teaism
400 Eighth Street NW; 638–6010
(see page 30 for full listing)

Hunan Chinatown
624 H Street; 738–5858
(see page 32 for full listing)

Go-Lo's
604 H Street; 347–4656
(see page 32 for full listing)

Fado
808 Seventh Street NW; 789–0066
(see page 33 for full listing)

Coco Loco
810 Seventh Street NW; 289–2626
(see page 33 for full listing)

Capitol Hill and Northeast

When Pierre L'Enfant was asked by George Washington to find a site for "the Congress House," he selected Jenkins Hill, an elevation with a commanding view of the future capital, a place he told Washington was "a pedestal waiting for a superstructure." Construction of the Capitol building began in 1793, when President Washington, wearing Masonic regalia, laid the building's cornerstone. The House and Senate wings were completed by 1803 and connected by a wooden bridge erected where the main building and great rotunda now stand. A 1930s guidebook to the District reports that the Hill was so rural in 1809 that, "the British Ambassador put up a covey of partridge" only 300 yards from the Capitol buildings. The unfinished Capitol was torched by the British during the War of 1812. Long story short, the two wings were reconstructed by 1826, but crowned with a low wooden dome; the huge, twin-shelled iron dome that you now see was completed in 1863 by President Lincoln, who saw its completion as symbolic of the survival of the Union.

The area around the Capitol, once you get past the monumental eastern fringe of the Supreme Court and the Library of Congress, is essentially the eighteenth- and nineteenth-century neighborhood that began as a collection of boardinghouses where representatives and senators lodged during congressional sessions. In fact, in 1793 Thomas Jefferson walked from one of those boardinghouses on New Jersey Avenue along the unpaved streets of the new capital to take his oath of office as president. The Hill, as Washingtonians call it, later became one of the city's prime residential areas, which accounts for the neighborhood's wonderful, large, and completely intact collection of fine homes that trace nineteenth-century residential architecture from antebellum Federal houses to Victorian-era Queen Annes.

Although young and youngish Hill staffers make up a large proportion of neighborhood residents, and crowd the streets during the day and on weekends, the area is surprisingly short of night life. The Hill's restaurant scene, aside from Union Station, is pretty much limited to the restaurant clusters along Pennsylvania Avenue SE and Massachusetts Avenue NE.

Capitol Hill and Northeast

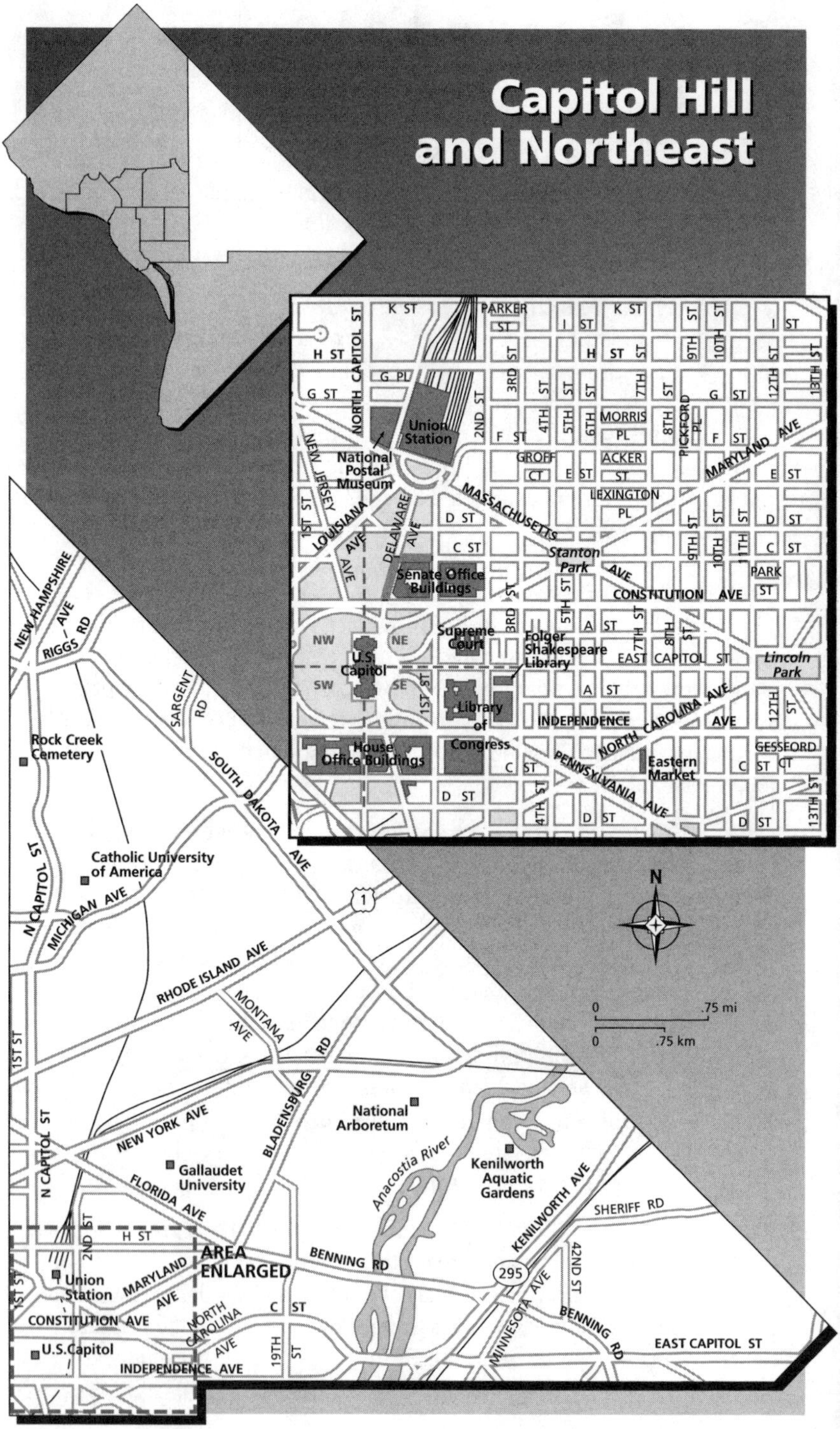
K ST
PARKER ST
I ST
H ST
G PL
G ST
NORTH CAPITOL ST
Union Station
National Postal Museum
NEW JERSEY
1ST ST
LOUISIANA AVE
DELAWARE AVE
2ND ST
3RD ST
4TH ST
5TH ST
6TH ST
7TH ST
8TH ST
9TH ST
10TH ST
11TH ST
12TH ST
13TH ST
MORRIS PL
PICKFORD PL
F ST
GROFF CT
ACKER ST
E ST
LEXINGTON PL
MARYLAND AVE
MASSACHUSETTS AVE
D ST
C ST
Stanton Park
PARK ST
Senate Office Buildings
CONSTITUTION AVE
NW
NE
SW
SE
U.S. Capitol
Supreme Court
Folger Shakespeare Library
A ST
EAST CAPITOL ST
Lincoln Park
Library of Congress
INDEPENDENCE AVE
NORTH CAROLINA AVE
House Office Buildings
GESSFORD CT
PENNSYLVANIA AVE
Eastern Market
N
0
.75 mi
0
.75 km
NEW HAMPSHIRE AVE
RIGGS RD
SARGENT RD
SOUTH DAKOTA AVE
Rock Creek Cemetery
Catholic University of America
N CAPITOL ST
MICHIGAN AVE
1
RHODE ISLAND AVE
MONTANA AVE
1ST ST
BLADENSBURG RD
NEW YORK AVE
National Arboretum
Anacostia River
Kenilworth Aquatic Gardens
Gallaudet University
FLORIDA AVE
KENILWORTH AVE
SHERIFF RD
H ST
2ND ST
AREA ENLARGED
BENNING RD
295
42ND ST
Union Station
MARYLAND AVE
CONSTITUTION AVE
NORTH CAROLINA AVE
C ST
19TH ST
MINNESOTA AVE
BENNING RD
EAST CAPITOL ST
U.S. Capitol
INDEPENDENCE AVE

CAPITOL HILL AND NORTHEAST

TOP ATTRACTIONS IN CAPITOL HILL AND NORTHEAST

Supreme Court

Union Station

Capital Children's Museum

National Postal Museum

Folger Shakespeare Library

Eastern Market

Library of Congress

Kenilworth Aquatic Gardens

Although visitor- and constituent-friendly Capitol Hill has been a major beneficiary of the District's steep decline in crime, you should still exercise the usual street smarts after dark.

Washington's **Union Station** is hardly off the beaten path; with 23 million visitors each year, it's the city's busiest site. Most visitors, however, pass through on their Amtrak trips to the District without taking a close look at this monumental Beaux Arts structure patterned after Rome's Baths of Diocletian, with its soaring, vaulted ceilings. In the magnificent main waiting room are forty-six elaborate statues of Roman legionnaires, one for each state in 1908, when this masterpiece opened. This glorious restoration has also become one of Washington's most vibrant places, where travelers and locals alike shop, take in a movie, buy a book at one of the five well-stocked bookstores, or dine at one of the station's forty restaurants and cafes. While lots of mangiare goes on in the twenty restaurants in the lower level food court, some of the better choices are upstairs on the main level and mezzanine.

When you see the Irish flag flying from the corner of North Capitol Street and F Street NW, it's not the Irish Embassy, but a corner of the old sod that's a lot more fun. Under the Hibernian tricolor is the **Phoenix Park Hotel,** which bills itself as the "center of Irish hospitality in America." Popular with lobbyists and tourists because of its prime location near Union Station, the Capitol, and the Union Station Metro stop, the hotel offers 150 upscale rooms and suites. Irish hospitality obviously extends downstairs: On the hotel's ground level is the **Dubliner Pub,** where the exuberant scene (ably assisted, if not inspired by Messrs. Guinness and Bass) attracts lots of Irish expats along with zillions of Irish wannabes. The fun really heats up every night at 9:00, when the live entertainment begins—sometimes professionals, sometimes customers who, after a few drinks, think that standing in front of an open mike and belting out "McNamara's Band" is perfectly normal. That might be you. Good pub food too, but nothing too fancy. Phoenix Park Hotel is located at 520 North Capitol Street; 638–6900 or (800) 824–5419, www.phoenixpark-hotel.com. Expensive. The Dubliner (737–3773), at the same address, is open Monday through Thursday 11:00 A.M. to 1:30 A.M., until 2:30 A.M. on the weekends. No reservations. Inexpensive.

As if this isn't enough flaunting of the green, next door to the Dubliner there's another Irish outpost, **Kelly's Irish Times,** at 14th and F Streets. A sign over Kelly's door invites "your thirsty, your famished, your befuddled masses" to drop in this no-nonsense pub with a formidable bar and a selection of sandwiches and salads. Open daily 11:00 A.M. to 2:00 A.M. Call 543–5433. Inexpensive.

You don't have to be a stamp collector to enjoy the **National Postal Museum,** located across from Union Station in what was once the former sorting room of Washington's City Post Office. The monumental post office building itself dates from 1914, but the museum only goes back to 1993, when it opened as part of the Smithsonian's network. In it you'll find exhibits that trace the history of America's mail system from its Colonial days down to the present.

A major crowd pleaser is the series of exhibits called *Moving the Mail,* tracing the growth of postal technology. It begins with a replica of a 1915 railway post office car, where clerks sorted letters and parcels to drop off at stations up the line; a film presents interviews with the few remaining post office veterans who worked in these cars. Next door a 1930 Ford Model A delivery vehicle painted in the old post office green illustrates how urban mail was delivered once it left those trains. Overhead, vintage planes from the U.S. Airmail Service hang from the ceiling to dramatize the beginnings of what is now the standard way of carrying the mail.

The museum is also the home of the Smithsonian's priceless collection of eleven million U.S. and foreign stamps, which can be viewed in a series of sliding vertical files. Your visit will probably end with a stop in the museum shop, which is crammed with books on stamps and stamp collecting, plus the usual branded mugs and T-shirts. The National Postal Museum, at First Street and Massachusetts Avenue NE (357-2991, www.si.edu/postal/collections/ustamp.htm), is open daily 10:00 A.M. to 5:30 P.M. One-hour tours begin weekdays at 11:00 A.M. and at 1:00 and 2:00 P.M.; weekend tours start at 11:00 A.M. and 2:00 P.M. For group tour information, call 357–2991. The museum also contains the world's largest philatelic research library; if you're a serious

Flying the Flag

*W*ould you like to have that flag flying over the U.S. Capitol for your very own? Ask your congressman or senator to order one from the Capitol's Flag Office, which will fly one from the building, then send it to you. It'll cost about $15, after which you can start building that shiny white dome for your house.

philatelist and want to visit, call 633–9370. The museum's Discovery Center has hands-on learning activities for children and adults on the third Saturday of every month.

The *Capital Children's Museum* is practically a must for anyone with small kids visiting Washington. Definitely located off the beaten path in a former church and convent behind Union Station, the museum brings together a number of educational and interactive exhibits that foster learning and teach children effortlessly about science, biology, and life in other lands. A big favorite is the Science Center, where budding scientists don goggles and lab coats to perform guided experiments in polymer making and biochemistry. In the interactive television studio, kids get on-camera experience at being a TV weather forecaster and in creating their own cartoons.

Among the biggest hits are the two exhibits that immerse children in Mexican and Japanese culture and life. In these national rooms children learn local crafts, cook basic dishes, and wander along typical streets in Mexico City and Tokyo; in the Japan rooms, children can even learn some basic Japanese and "ride" one of Japan's famed bullet trains. Capital Children's Museum, 800 Third Street NE (675–4120, www.ccm.org), is perfect for group visits, so if you're in Washington with other families, call 675–4149 or e-mail reservations@ccm.org for information about group rates. Admission is $6.00 per person, $4.00 for seniors. Open every day 10:00 A.M. to 5:00 P.M., until 6:00 P.M. Easter through Labor Day; closed the entire week after Labor Day. Metro: Union Station (red line).

When visiting the *Supreme Court,* most visitors troop through the first floor and the tours that go to the building's courtroom, America's ultimate judicial chamber, for a potted lecture. Be sure to visit the lower level, however, to see lively exhibits that document the building's fascinating history and its architectural evolution; other displays recount the gypsy nature of the Court, which had no home to call its own for 146 years until this imposing Greek marble temple was opened in 1935. In the Court's theater, also downstairs, every half hour between 9:00 A.M. and 4:00 P.M., you can watch a twenty-four-minute film about its operations and proceedings. Around the corner there's a gift shop selling legal lore, including law books, judicial neckties, and other Court marginalia. Best of all, you'll also find on this level a reasonably priced cafeteria and elaborate snack bar, with good food and (naturally) the most dignified surroundings of any federal government eatery. The Supreme Court building itself is at First Street NE; 479–3000. Open 9:00 A.M. to 4:30 P.M. Monday through Friday; closed Saturday and Sunday. The building's cafeteria is open Monday through Friday 7:30 to 10:30 A.M. and 11:30 A.M. to 2:00 P.M. The snack bar's hours are Monday through Friday 10:30 A.M. to 3:30 P.M. The gift shop is open Monday through Friday 9:00 A.M. to 4:25 P.M. Metro stop: Union Station (red line).

When the Supreme Court is in session, beginning on the first Monday in October and ending in April, you can sit in on the one-hour oral arguments the justices will hear in each case. Oral arguments are conducted on Mondays, Tuesdays, and Wednesdays for two weeks each month. To hear them, join one of the two lines that form in front of the Court steps before sessions begin at 10:00 A.M. One is for legal buffs who want to attend an entire argument; the other is a "three-minute line" for those satisfied with a brief look at the proceedings. Seating for these events is on a first-come, first-served basis and begins at 9:30 A.M., so you need to get in line well before that. To see what's scheduled when you're in town, consult the Court schedules in the first section of *The Washington Post.*

The **Sewall-Belmont House** is one of Capitol Hill's oldest and best examples of Federal architecture and one of the top women's history sites in the United States. The small original house on this site, built in 1750, was expanded into the current mansion in 1800 by Robert Sewall, and is now its rear wing and kitchen. Because American snipers fired from it on their commanding general, British troops burned the house during the War of 1812, the only private home in Washington to suffer that fate. After rebuilding, Sewall-Belmont House was home to many distinguished officials, including Albert Gallatin, secretary of the treasury under Jefferson and Monroe, who may have worked out details of the Louisiana Purchase in the house's front rooms, as well as a slew of U.S. senators. In 1929 the house became the headquarters of the National Women's Party, the militant wing of the feminist movement founded by Alice Paul, the radical strategist who led hunger strikes and marches and, in 1923, drafted the Equal Rights Amendment on a desk displayed in this house.

The house's feminist library contains a vast and valuable collection of suffragist archives and exhibits celebrating women's history; its rooms are filled with mementos of the early days of the suffrage movement. Your guide will also show you *We Were Arrested, Of Course,* a film chronicling the days before the Nineteenth Amendment passed in 1920. In those days, not only was a woman's right to vote controversial, but insisting on it could land you in the cooler. At the Sewall-Belmont House you'll also look in on some historic rooms, including an elegant front parlor straight out of 1880, with Victorian gilt mirrors, period furniture, and a square 1875 piano. There's also a small gift shop. The Sewall-Belmont House, 144 Constitution Avenue NE, has guided tours Tuesday through Friday at 11:00 A.M., noon, and 1:00 and 2:00 P.M., Saturday at noon, 1:00, 2:00 and 3:00 P.M. Call 546–3989, fax 546–3997, or visit www.natwomanparty.org. Contributions are appreciated. Metro: Union Station (red line).

Inside a classic art deco building across from the Supreme Court, the **Folger Shakespeare Library** is possibly the world's greatest collection of works by and about William Shakespeare. The library and its collection of priceless artifacts, along with the Folger's Elizabethan Theater and the Folger Consort, with its regular programs of early English music, constitute one of the capital's greatest cultural and intellectual treasures. The much praised facade of the building is worth examining for its carved motifs from Shakespeare's plays.

You'll experience a major time shift beyond that 1930s facade when you enter sixteenth-century England in the Folger's majestic Great Hall, inspired by a grand and historic room of Brasenose College, Oxford. The hall's oak-paneled walls and its high, vaulted ceiling display Shakespeare's coat of arms plus motifs from his plays that the docents call "hints and clues." The Great Hall is also the exhibition space for rare items from Shakespeare's era and artifacts of his work from the Folger's own collections. During my visit the exhibit subject was "Fortune," a favorite theme of Shakespeare and his contemporaries; the displays included sixteenth-century playing cards and other ancient gambling

Holiday Concerts

*I*f you're in Washington on Memorial Day, July 4, or Labor Day, be sure to attend the National Symphony's gala holiday concert on the West Lawn of the Capitol. Concerts start at 8:00 P.M., but most people arrive well before that with a blanket and a picnic supper. Prepare for a real patriotic surge and an intensely patriotic experience by tucking a few flags into your hamper.

Mother's Day Tour

A number of those wonderful Federal row houses you'll see on Capitol Hill and their elaborate gardens are open to the public every Mother's Day weekend on the annual "Capitol Hill Restoration Society House and Garden Tour." The tour begins Saturday evening with a Candlelight Tour from 5:00 to 8:00 P.M., then continues on Sunday with open houses from noon to 5:00 P.M. Also on Sunday there's a reception from 3:00 to 6:00 P.M. at the Folger Library, which is a Capitol Hill "must" in itself. Jitneys will take you from house to house. Tickets are $15 in advance and can be purchased at Eastern Market and other Hill locations or by writing to the Restoration Society at P.O. Box 15264, Washington, D.C. 20003-0264. If you wait until the day of the tour you'll pay $20. Call 543–0425 for more information.

devices. Another case contained the only known first folio of *Titus Andronicus*. The Elizabethan Theater, where the Folger stages educational symposia and an annual cycle of Shakespeare plays, is a timbered replica of an inn yard theater of Shakespeare's day.

Before leaving, check out the Folger's spiffy little museum store, with lots of books and plays by and about the bard. For information about the Folger's many programs, including the consort and theater schedules, call 544–7077. The Folger, at 201 East Capitol Street SE (544–4600; www.folger.edu) is open Monday through Saturday 10:00 A.M. to 4:00 P.M. Tours of the Folger Rooms and Architecture are given Monday through Friday at 11:00 A.M., Saturday at 11:00 A.M. and 1:00 P.M. Tours of the garden are given every third Saturday from April through October, at 10:00 and 11:00 A.M. Metro: Capitol South (orange and blue lines) or Union Station (red line).

After leaving the Folger, turn right and saunter along East Capitol Street to get an idea of Capitol Hill as a neighborhood. Heading toward Lincoln Park, you'll pass an eclectic mix of ornate Victorian row houses, Federal beauties from the Hill's earliest days, and even a sprinkling of Washington's first apartment houses, most of them dating back to Victorian times. To make this stroll even more pleasant, most houses have handsome front yards with gardens, trees, and benches for sitting and gazing.

East Capitol Street's small-town feel includes local shops from another era, especially **Grubb's Pharmacy,** at East Capitol and Fourth Street NE, which, like much of this neighborhood, could have been marooned in a 1900s time warp. Grubb's resembles an old-time general store more than a pharmacy, piled high with medical equipment and supplies of every imaginable kind, plus a huge stock of homeopathic remedies. Grubb's (543–4400) is open Monday through Friday 9:00 A.M. to 7:00 P.M., Saturday 9:00 A.M. to 3:00 P.M.; closed Sunday.

Arriving at Lincoln Park, a neighborhood hangout for dogs and families, you'll see two great statues: the 1876 *Emancipation Monument,* a statue of Abraham Lincoln holding the Emancipation Proclamation, and an imposing one of black activist and educator Mary McLeod Bethune.

In 1871, Frederick Douglass, already distinguished for his writings, his memoirs about his life as a slave, and his wartime role as close adviser to President Lincoln on African-American matters, moved from Rochester, New York, and bought a home on Capitol Hill. His first home in the District is now a small and highly interesting house museum, the **Frederick Douglass Museum and Hall of Fame for Caring Americans.**

The front parlor, Douglass's former study, is a wonderful re-creation of an upper-class Washington parlor of the period. The room contains Douglass's violin, comfortable chairs, and a writing desk with some of his papers, including his "freed man" papers signed by Lincoln and an invitation to the dedication ceremonies for the Washington Monument. Next door, in the dining room/library, the walls are lined with photographs and mementos of people important to Douglass, such as Booker T. Washington, Harriet Tubman, and Sojourner Truth. Near the original fireplace, which was uncovered during restoration, you'll see the "Paper of Manumission," which gave Douglass his freedom, and an 1863 safe conduct pass, signed by Lincoln, allowing him to pass through Union lines on missions for the president. Douglass moved to Cedar Hill, his Anacostia home, in 1878 (see the Waterfront and Anacostia chapter).

The back half of the ground floor and the upstairs bedrooms are devoted to photographs of and awards to "caring Americans" who have distinguished themselves through their good works in helping others and in their philanthropic activities.

The Frederick Douglass Museum and Hall of Fame for Caring Americans, 316-320 A Street NE (547–4273, www.caring-institute.org/fdm/fdm.html), is open Monday, Wednesday, and Friday from noon to 2:00 P.M. Metro: Capitol South (orange and blue lines).

Great Ideas from the Folger

Among the best-selling items at the Folger Library's excellent gift shop are mugs and T-shirts bearing the popular Shakespeare quote "The first thing we do, let's kill all the lawyers." And this just across the street from the Supreme Court?

"Outside of the killings, Washington has one of the lowest crime rates in the country."

—*Mayor Marion Barry*

Although the **Library of Congress,** the world's largest library, is definitely not an off-the-beaten-path destination, many of its visitors probably don't take full advantage of its numerous exhibitions, concerts, and lectures. Film buffs shouldn't overlook the free showings of classic films from the library's enormous film archive in the Mary Pickford Theater. To get an idea about what's available, including the superb special and permanent exhibits, check out the twelve-minute orientation film, then take one of the four full tours of the Jefferson Building that begin Monday through Saturday at 11:30 A.M. and 1:00, 2:30, and 4:00 P.M.

The facade of the library's main building is inspired by the Paris Opera House, which makes it a bit grandiose for some critics. But the interior, with its grand staircase and the octagonal main reading room, excites the admiration of every visitor, even stodgy Henry James, who pronounced it "magnificent."

It's the Jefferson Building that gets all the attention, but you might, especially around lunchtime, consider crossing Independence Avenue to visit the Library's newish **Madison Building,** at the corner of First Street and Independence Avenue SE. On the sixth floor you'll find one of the best government cafeterias in town, with good food, plenty of space, and a fabulous panoramic view over southeast Washington and northern Virginia. The cafeteria is open Monday through Friday 9:00 to 10:30 A.M. and 12:30 to 3:00 P.M. The Madison Building also has an excellent gift shop, where the emphasis is on American history and literature. Open Monday through Saturday 9:30 A.M. to 5:00 P.M.

High on my list of candidates for the city's most glorious church is **St. Mark's Episcopal Church,** built in 1888 and located at Third and A Streets SE, behind the Library of Congress's Adams Building. The tall, high-ceilinged nave of this Romanesque beauty is lined with exposed red brick that makes a simple background for a dazzling collection of stained glass windows, including a splendid Louis Tiffany masterpiece in the baptistry at the north end. A colorful cross made from children's drawings hangs from the nave's beamed ceiling. If St. Mark's is locked, ask at Baxter House, the church offices at 118 Third Street SE and someone will show you around.

If you've been missing those terrific European food halls where glistening fish and artistic cuts of meat vie for attention with geometric displays of fruit, exotic cheeses, and vegetables, you'll enjoy visiting the

Hill Street Mews

*C*apitol Hill is also where you can still find some of Washington's famous (or notorious) alleys, which were built into the original city plan to provide tradesmen with backdoor access to substantial homes and mansions. But after the Civil War, the alleys became festering slums where freed slaves squatted and worked under substandard conditions. Some of the few remaining alleys have now been gentrified and turned into smart mews homes for the affluent. Georgetown's Pomander Walk is a good example, but on the Hill, three of the best examples of alleys that have become tiny, tony streets, are Miller's Court, which you can find by following the directional sign in front of the Douglass House at 316 A Street NE, Rumsey Court, off D Street SE, opposite the exit from the Capitol South Metro station, and Terrace Court, just off A Street behind the Supreme Court. Another hidden beauty is Library Court, reachable by the alley next to 315 A Street SE, just behind the Library of Congress's Adams Building.

Eastern Market, 225 Seventh Street SE (between C Street and North Carolina Avenue). To see Eastern Market's food pageant at its peak, go early on Saturday morning, when trucks packed with crates of fresh produce, game, fish, and meats roll in from Virginia farms and Chesapeake Bay, followed closely by finicky buyers from some of Washington's top restaurants. Eastern Market is open Tuesday to Saturday 7:00 A.M. to 6:00 P.M., Sunday 9:00 A.M. to 4:00 P.M. Metro stop for the Market and its neighbors? Why it's Eastern Market on the orange and blue lines.

Folks from this neighborhood usually head for the market's specialty food shops like the Union Meat Co., for its meats and half smokes on a bun, or the Fine Sweete Shoppe. But truckers, locals, and tourists alike usually end up at *The Market Lunch,* a stools-and-paper-plates cafeteria famous for crab cakes, fried oysters, and shrimp, along with immense breakfasts that would horrify your cardiologist. Open Tuesday through Saturday 7:30 A.M. to 3:00 P.M.

But the market is more than just food; this redbrick food hall and its surrounding stores and stands is also the epicenter of Capitol Hill social and cultural life, especially in the market's north wing, which is given over to exhibits of crafts, wearable art, and jewelry by neighborhood artists and artisans. Outside, surrounding the market building, you'll find a bustling combination of vegetable market and flea market, with vendors selling an eclectic mix of everything from prints, clothing, and jewelry to apple pie and flowers. Across Seventh Street there's an even larger flea market that fills a large playground every Saturday and Sunday.

The Market Lunch

This vibrant neighborhood also boasts a first-class used book store. *Capitol Hill Books,* at 657 C Street SE, is stacked high with books of every vintage and description and literally overflows with language books, which are located in the shop's lavatory. Cookbooks, naturally, are filed in the kitchen sink of this former row house, but owner Jim Toole's excellent collection of District of Columbia history and books on American politics are shelved right out front by the counter. Open Monday through Friday 11:30 A.M. to 6:00 P.M., weekends 9:00 A.M. to 6:00 P.M. Call 544–1621.

For some historic booze and bistro food with a Cajun twist, head for *Tunnicliff's,* across from the Market at 222 Seventh Street SE. Tunnicliff's has been functioning on Capitol Hill in one form or another ever since William Tunnicliff opened the Eastern Branch Hotel 2 blocks away in 1796. The sense of D.C. history is never far away, especially when you see the framed copy of an 1850 memo from Senators Jefferson Davis and Sam Houston inviting their senatorial colleagues to join them at Tunnicliff's for a discussion of flogging in the Navy. There's live Cajun music or jazz on Saturday night; brunch on Saturday and Sunday. Tunnicliff's kitchen is open Monday through Friday noon to 11:00 P.M., Saturday 11:00 A.M. to 11:00 P.M., and Sunday 11:00 A.M. to 10:00 P.M. The ever-lively bar, however, is open much later every night and until 3:00 on Sunday mornings. Call 546–3663 or visit www.tunnicliffs.com. No floggings please—it disturbs the drinkers. Inexpensive.

Antiques on the Hill, across the street from the Eastern Market at 701 Independence Avenue SE is one of the area's best places to find just the lamp or antique table you've been coveting. You can join half of Capitol Hill in rummaging through this storefront crammed with secondhand treasures Tuesday through Sunday between 11:00 A.M. and 5:30 P.M. Call 543–1819.

Leaving the market, a right turn will take you to *Woven History,* worth seeing even if your interest in fine rugs and carpets is only minimal. The shop has a wide selection of dazzling vegetable-dyed hand-spun wool carpets made in Pakistan by refugees from Afghanistan, Tibet, and Nepal, along with other carpets imported from Turkey and Azerbaijan. Its companion shop, *Silk Road,* under the same management, specializes in exquisite woven goods and tribal and village arts and crafts from all along the route of Asia's fabled Silk Road. These shops "two treasures, one gate," are located at 311-315 Seventh Street SE. Open Tuesday through Sunday 10:00 A.M. to 6:00 P.M. Call 543–1705 or visit www.wovenhistory.com.

This block also contains one of Capitol Hill's most popular restaurants, *Bluestone Cafe,* 327 Seventh Street SE, where the courses all seem to be in the category of American comfort food: corn soup, crab cakes, steaks, and massive salads. The same goes for the funky decor, with polished wood furniture, fruit prints on the walls, and, for some reason, a red cement floor. Open for lunch Tuesday through Friday 11:30 A.M. to 2:30 P.M. and for brunch Saturday and Sunday 11:00 A.M. to 3:00 P.M. Dinner hours are Monday through Thursday 5:30 to 10:00 P.M., until 10:30 on weekends. Call 547–9007.

When you proceed down Seventh Street to the corner of Pennsylvania Avenue, you'll be standing in front of *Bread and Chocolate,* the local outpost of a highly successful Washington group that serves specialty coffees, great pastry, and sandwiches. Bread and Chocolate is also famous for its Sunday brunch and its daily breakfasts, where you'd be well advised to throw dietary caution to the wind and order the divine French toast. Bread and Chocolate, 666 Pennsylvania Avenue SE (547–2875), is open Monday through Saturday 7:00 A.M. to 7:00 P.M., Sunday 8:00 A.M. to 6:00 P.M.

To get an idea of the Hill's creative life and talent, visit the *Capitol Hill Art League Gallery,* at 545 Seventh Street SE, which sponsors a practically nonstop program of juried exhibits of paintings, photographs, and mixed media; gallery talks and lectures usually accompany each show. The Art League also offers a program of art classes. Open Monday through Friday 9:00 A.M. to 8:00 P.M., Saturday 10:00 A.M. to 2:00 P.M. Call 547–6839 for exhibit information or check out www.chaw.org.

The Eastern Market neighborhood also includes one of Washington's liveliest specialty stores and a must for anyone interested in the performing arts. **Backstage,** at 545 Eighth Street SE (544–5744), is D.C.'s showbiz equipment headquarters, with a large repertoire of ready-made costumes and wigs for sale or rent, theatrical books and scripts, stage makeup, and theatrical posters too. Open Monday through Saturday 11:00 A.M. to 7:00 P.M., Sunday noon to 5:00 P.M.

Although the Capitol Hill area includes all four of the city's quadrants, it is also the gateway to the Northeast section, which includes the community known as Brookland. The Northeast is itself diverse, ranging from quiet suburban streets to gritty industrial districts, but it is also, in its Brooklands neighborhood, about the closest thing you'll find to Vatican on the Potomac. About sixty Catholic organizations cluster in Brooklands, which is said to be the highest number in one area outside of Rome; the most significant structure is the **Basilica of the National Shrine of the Immaculate Conception.**

As soon as you spot the Basilica's brightly colored mosaic dome, flanked by a bell tower that seems straight out of Venice's Piazza San Marco, you know that you're in a special place where the operative word is "immense." This is the largest Catholic church in the hemisphere: It can hold 6,000 worshipers in its upper church and 400 in the crypt below, which is mod-

Statuary Symbolism

*T*hat statue atop the Capitol dome is **Freedom,** cast from a plaster model that sculptor Thomas Crawford made in Rome, but not after considerable political flak. Crawford had originally designed a simple cloth covering for Freedom's head called a Phrygian cap, which was an ancient symbol of freed slaves, who used them to cover their shaved heads. This did not sit well with Secretary of War Jefferson Davis, future President of the Confederacy, who was not exactly a fan of liberated slaves, even symbolically. Crawford was compelled to trade the cap for a crested Roman battle helmet, representing America's victory over tyranny.

After a near-sinking on the way from Italy, the 19-foot statue was set in place in December 1863 as the final touch on the dome, which Lincoln had insisted be completed, despite the Civil War, as a symbol of the continuing Union. If you see the lantern just below Freedom lit, it means that the House or the Senate are in night session.

eled after the Roman catacombs. This magnificent church, rich in marble mosaics, is a mix of the Byzantine and the Romanesque, with thirty-two chapels in the upper church that gleam with the vivid colors of their 200 stained glass windows. The effect of the interior can be overwhelming, so don't forget to look in on the Basilica's quiet gardens, especially the restful Mary's Garden, all in white with restful pools and fountains.

The shrine also has an excellent gift shop and bookstore, plus a cafeteria, which can come in handy in this restaurant-free zone. The Basilica of the National Shrine of the Immaculate Conception, 400 Michigan Avenue NE (526–8300, www.nationalshrine.com), is open daily 7:00 A.M. to 7:00 P.M. Mass is celebrated several times a day. Guided tours are given Sundays from 1:30 to 4:00 P.M. and weekdays from 9:00 to 11:00 A.M. and 1:00 to 3:00 P.M. The cafeteria is open from 7:30 A.M. to 2:00 P.M. (until 3:00 on Sunday). If you're interested in a group tour—and there are a lot of them at this national shrine—call 526–8300 and ask for the Pilgrimage Department. Metro: Brookland (red line).

A much lesser known feature of Northeast's "Little Rome" is the *Franciscan Monastery*—modeled on the famed Hagia Sofia church in Istanbul—where Franciscan priests and brothers are trained for work protecting the Holy Land's religious sites and helping its needy. You don't have to spring for a passport or become a martyr to jet lag to visit the Holy Sepulcher or the Grotto of Bethlehem. They, along with reproductions of other Holy Land shrines like the grotto of Gethsemane, are right here in little old Washington, in the monastery's lush rose gardens. There's also a detailed and spooky reproduction of a frescoed Roman catacomb to give you an idea of what early worshipers were up against in the real Rome. The Franciscan Monastery, 1400 Quincy Street NE (526–6800) is open daily 9:00 A.M. to 5:00 P.M. daily. Tours by Franciscan brothers are given Monday through Saturday on the hour (except at noon) from 9:00 A.M. to 4:00 P.M., and hourly on Sunday from 1:00 to 4:00 P.M. The gift shop is open daily 9:00 A.M. to 5:00 P.M.

The warm and cozy *Cup of Dreams,* at 3629 Twelfth Street NE, is just the place to grab a cappuccino or bagel after your visit to the Franciscan Monastery. The atmosphere in this neighborhood coffeehouse will take you back to the pre-Starbucks era, when folks gathered in local coffee shops for poetry readings and large doses of cool jazz. At the Cup you might also run into local folk singers and musicians giving impromptu concerts. It's that kind of a place. Cup of Dreams is open Monday through Wednesday 6:00 A.M. to 9:30 P.M., Thursday 6:00 A.M. to 5:00 P.M., and Saturday 8:00 A.M. to 5:00 P.M. Call 526–6562. Metro: Brookland (red line).

One of the mid-Atlantic's dance meccas is **Dance Place,** a 200-seat center of contemporary and avant-garde dance. Every weekend, all year long, Dance Place presents programs of original, often experimental dance by top American and international companies. Every June it hosts a "Dance Africa Festival" that attracts large numbers of African and African-American dancers and dance lovers. During the day, Dance Place offers a number of modern and African dance classes for children and adults. Dance Place is located at 3225 Eighth Street NE. Call 269–1600 or visit www.danceplace.org. Metro: Brookland (red line).

Even if your interest in flowers surfaces only every Valentine's Day, you'll have to agree that the **U.S. National Arboretum** is one of Washington's "must visit" sites. The Arboretum, which is run by the U.S. Department of Agriculture as a research and education facility and as a living museum, is located on the city's outskirts, not far from an industrial zone and the high-octane, high-decibel roar of New York Avenue, a.k.a. U.S. 50. But once inside this 444-acre mini state, there's a great sense of beauty and tranquillity.

Most of the Arboretum's main attractions are reachable via the 10 miles of roadways within the park, but start off at the Administration Building for a map, then stroll outside to begin your tour at a large pond dense with lilies, where kids are feeding some of the biggest koi you've ever seen. Move on to the National Herb Garden, with its $2^1/_2$ acres of 800 herbs, including lavender, sweet bay trees, rosemary, and a formal sixteenth-century knot garden with dwarf evergreens. Visiting the National Bonsai and Penjing Museum, a few steps away, is like entering a corner of Asia, where quiet gardens with stone lanterns showcase ferns, chrysanthemums, and a superb collection of bonsai trees from Japan, China, and North America. The North American contingent is made up of miniature cypress, cedar, and juniper, while the Asian pavilions are lined with 200-year-old yews and wisteria. The area's "Special Exhibits Wing" is located in a Chinese house with an exquisite Chinese scholar's studio in the style of the sixteenth century; nearby you'll find row after row of splashy bonsai azaleas.

You can continue by car or "tram tour" to the outlying displays, such as the dogwood, azalea, and conifer collections; check at the information desk to see which are in flower during your visit. Picnicking is possible at the Arboretum in either the National Grove of State Trees picnic area or in the area behind the gift shop.

No matter where you go, you can't miss the National Capitol Columns, the twenty-two Corinthian columns that from 1826 to 1957 formed the

Legislative Lunching

*I*f it's noon and you don't know where your senator or representative is, it's a pretty good bet you'll find him or her schmoozing with other politicos or, heaven forbid, even those satanic lobbyists, at one of two restaurants where more decisions than you'd like to think are made over top-notch food.

• **The Monocle,** *107 D Street NE; 546–4488. The atmosphere here is strictly old-time Capitol Hill, with signed photos of national luminaries and walls bearing famous political quotes like, "I give special consideration to everybody," and "Washington is the only city where sound travels faster than light." This is where our nation's lawgivers gather for power breakfasts and lunches or dinners of crab cakes, filets, rib eyes, and large salads. Jack Kennedy liked the roast beef so much that, after becoming president, he regularly sent a limo* over for sandwiches, making the Monocle, according to one wit, "JFK's favorite pickup place." Open Monday through Friday only from 11:30 A.M. to Midnight. Expensive. Metro: Union Station (red line).

• **La Colline,** *400 N. Capitol Street NW; 737–0400. One of the city's top French restaurants, with or without the congressional crowd. This warm and inviting bistro serves up great seafood and vegetable dishes, along with a super duck l'orange. Ravioli stuffed with wild mushrooms is another good choice, as are French standbys like cassoulet and choucroute garni. And if you like foie gras, this one's for you. Desserts are exceptional. Reservations a must. Open Monday through Friday 7:00 to 10:00 A.M. and 11:30 A.M. to 3:00 P.M., Monday through Saturday 6:00 to 10:00 P.M. Expensive. Metro: Union Station (red line).*

East portico of the Capitol building. These columns, which looked down on the Jackson and Lincoln inaugurations, were dismantled when the building's east front was extended; they were stored at the Arboretum until 1990 when they were reerected in their former configuration.

The U.S. National Arboretum, 3501 New York Avenue NE (245–2726, www.ars-grin.gov/ars/Beltsville/na), is open as follows: grounds 8:00 A.M. to 5:00 P.M.; Bonsai and Penjing Museum, 10:00 A.M. to 3:30 P.M.; Administration Building, 8:00 A.M. to 4:30 P.M. weekdays and 9:00 A.M. to 5:00 P.M. weekends; gift shop, 10:00 A.M. to 3:30 P.M. weekdays and 10:30 A.M. to 5:00 P.M. weekends. Tram Tours, the Arboretum's sightseeing trains, run from mid-April to mid-October, weekends only; tours leave at 10:30 and 11:30 A.M. and 1:00, 2:00, 3:00, and 4:00 P.M. No Metro nearby; travel by car or taxi. If you're driving, the Arboretum is reached by taking New York Avenue from the city, then following the directional sign posted just past the intersection of New York Avenue and Bladensburg Road. Because its headquarters is located very near the Arboretum's gate, Yellow Cab (544–1212) is probably the best bet for a return trip by taxi.

When you visit the **Kenilworth Aquatic Gardens,** you're standing in the District's ultimate off-the-beaten-path experience, a unique nature sanctuary that few Washingtonians have visited or even heard of. The gardens consist of twelve acres and forty-five ponds located on the wetlands of the Anacostia River, Washington's last tidal marsh and home to exotic water lilies, ferns, and lotuses; it is the only National Park Service installation devoted entirely to water plants. The gardens are also a sanctuary for a large variety of birds (including the occasional bald eagle), wetland animals from turtles to snakes and fish, which have returned in force, thanks to herculean efforts to restore the once-dead Anacostia.

As you enter you'll be tempted to go no farther, choosing instead to plop down on the porch of the nifty little visitor center and enjoy the vast ponds with lily pads, lavender water hyacinth, and primrose, all surrounded by carpets of daffodils. But press on to follow the Marsh River Trail back into the wetlands and see the riverside sites where fox, muskrat, and deer hang out and wading herons often appear among the cattails. Ranger-led tours are also available, but you must reserve in advance. Field guides and other nature publications are available at the visitor center. Kenilworth Aquatic Gardens, 1900 Anacostia Avenue NE (426–6905, www.nps.gov/nace/keaq), are open 8:00 A.M. to 4:00 P.M. There are no Metro stops or bus lines that service the Gardens. Because of potential security problems, take a cab or your own vehicle to the Gardens.

You're probably too young to have seen an idyllic, vintage 1870 college campus, but if you ever want to know exactly what one looked like, get in your time machine and warp yourself over to **Gallaudet University,** America's preeminent institution for the hearing impaired. There, at 800 Florida Avenue NE, you'll find, preserved like a fly in amber, a glorious collection of Victorian Gothic and Queen Anne houses gathered around a campus with grounds and gardens designed by Frederick Law Olmsted, the same nineteenth-century landscape architect who planned Central Park and dozens of other landscape masterworks.

Aside from its aesthetics and being the world's only university for the deaf, Gallaudet has a distinction that will never die as long as there are sports trivia nuts. In the nineteenth-century, Gallaudet football players noticed that opposing teams were reading and anticipating all of their plays, which were exchanged among the players in sign language. To thwart this, the team began gathering in a tight circle to sign plays without being observed, thereby inventing the football huddle.

The campus visitor center (651–5000, www.gallaudet.edu) is open Monday through Friday 9:00 A.M. to 5:00 P.M. and offers tours. To get there either drive or take a D-2, D-4, or D-6 bus from downtown.

If you're in the Gallaudet neighborhood, find out what an Italian mega-grocery looks like by heading for *Litteri's,* located among the loading docks and warehouses of the Capital City Market, where the city's foods are brought and traded. At Litteri's you'll find Washington's oldest, largest, and best Italian grocery. It's a treat for the eyes and nose, and a still life of all goodies Italian, from shimmering bottles of extra virgin olive oil to thirty brands of balsamic vinegar and every known pasta shape. In the back, a deli counter serves up sandwiches, hunks of Romano and provolone cheese, and glistening slices of prosciutto. Just walking through Litteri's will cost you 300 calories, but it will save you a trip to Rome. Litteri's is at 517 Morse Street NE, near the intersection of New York and Florida Avenues. Open Tuesday and Wednesday 8:00 A.M. to 4:00 P.M., Thursday and Friday until 5:00 P.M., and Saturday until 3:00 P.M. Call 244–0183. Drive or take a D-2, D-4, or D-6 bus from downtown.

PLACES TO STAY IN CAPITOL HILL AND NORTHEAST

Bull Moose B&B, 101 Fifth Street NE; 547–1050 or (800) 261–2768, guesthse.com/caphill/index. html. In case you're wondering, the Bull Moose in question is the breakaway third party founded by Teddy Roosevelt in the early twentieth century. T. R. would have felt right at home in this turreted Victorian mansion with high ceilings and lots of wood paneling. The Bull Moose's eighteen guest rooms all have Rooseveltian themes. The "Kermit Room," named for his son, is decorated in early twentieth-century safari style with weathered gladstone bags stacked in a corner. Other rooms also echo the President who inspired the "Teddy bear" (there are a few of them around as well). Inexpensive. Metro stops: Union Station (red line) or Capitol South (orange and blue), but it's about a 6- or 7-block walk from each.

Capitol Hill Suites, 200 C Street SE; 543–6000, fax 547–2608. It's not just a great location—a two-minute walk from the Capitol and the Supreme Court, and across the street from the Library of Congress—that makes this former apartment house so appealing. The 152 suites, studios, and efficiencies, each with a kitchen or cooking facilities, were all remodeled in mid-2000 and the prices are moderate. Judging from the photos and endorsements that line the lobby walls, this is also a big favorite of the congressmen who work just across the street. Moderate. Metro stop: Capitol South (orange and blue lines).

Hotel George, 15 E Street NW; 347–4200 or (800) 576–8331, www.hotel george.com. The sleek, contemporary lobby of glass and stainless steel is your introduction to a boutique-chic, New Yorky world of neomodern rooms and dramatic paintings by Steve Kaufman, a disciple of Andy Warhol. The George's 139 rooms offer intimacy and style along with state-of-the-art in-room communications with the outside world. Downstairs, the George's hip French bistro restaurant, Bis, is in a class by itself; reservations are a must, especially for the memorable Sunday brunch. This all comes at a price, but the George offers some surprisingly low weekend deals. Expensive. Metro stop: Union Station (red line).

PLACES TO EAT IN CAPITOL HILL AND NORTHEAST

Aatish, 609 Pennsylvania Avenue SE; 544–0931. This storefront near Eastern Market is a neighborhood favorite for its fresh, well-prepared Pakistani dishes, its relaxed, friendly atmosphere, and its low prices. Try the clay oven chicken or shrimp tandooris (my personal favorite: the shrimp kebab tandoori). Open Monday through Thursday

11:30 A.M. to 2:30 P.M. and 5:00 to 10:00 P.M., until 10:30 on Friday and Saturday. Inexpensive. Metro stop: Eastern Market (orange and blue lines).

B. Smith's, Union Station; 289–6188. Located in the station's former Presidential waiting room, this restaurant is a luxurious reminder of the days when Presidents traveled only by train. The watchword here is Southern cooking—jambalaya, deep-fried catfish, fried green tomatoes, and a potent seafood gumbo. Feeling adventurous? Order the "Swamp Thing," a wonderful dish of mustardy mixed seafood over collard greens. Try the desserts before you waddle over to your train. Open Monday through Friday 11:30 A.M. to 4:00 P.M. and 5:00 to 10:00 P.M., Saturday 11:30 A.M. to 4:00 P.M. for brunch and evenings 5:00 P.M. to 1:00 A.M., Sunday brunch 11:30 A.M. to 3:00 P.M. and dinner is 3:00 to 9:00 P.M. Expensive.

Where to Find the Author's Favorite Places to Stay in Capitol Hill and Northeast

Phoenix Park Hotel
*520 North Capitol Street; 638–6900
or (800) 824–5419
(see page 39 for full listing)*

America, Union Station; 682–9555. Everyone wants to be in America, which sports a large menu of regional specialties from all over the United States, including New Mexico's Navaho fry bread, Cincinnati's chili, and Cobb salad, first produced in Hollywood. There's even something called a fluffernutter sandwich from Las Vegas, which I'm not sure I'll ever order. And is the Reuben sandwich really a "Nebraska specialty"? What happened to the lower East Side? Open Monday through Friday 11:30 A.M. to midnight, until 1:00 A.M. on the weekends. Moderate.

East Street Cafe, Union Station; 371–6788. This bright and cheerful cafe, on the station's mezzanine level, calls itself "A culinary journey of the East" because of its offerings of tempuras, curries, Pad Thai, and other classics from eight Asian nations, including seldom seen dishes from Malaysia. If you're in a hurry, try a one-meal noodle or rice dish.

Open Monday through Friday 11:00 A.M. to 9:00 P.M., Saturday noon to 9:00 P.M., and Sunday 1:00 to 8:00 P.M. Moderate.

Thunder Grill, Union Station; 898–0051. Decorated in adobe and turquoise, Thunder Grill offers classic Southwestern U.S. dishes such as burritos, fajitas, and tacos, along with the house specialty, chicken enchiladas with mole sauce. You'll also be offered a wide selection of margaritas served by the yard in a 48-ounce glass, after which you may not even care about getting on that train. Open daily 11:30 A.M. to 10:00 P.M. Moderate.

Cafe Berlin, 322 Massachusetts Avenue NE; 543–7656. One of Washington's few German restaurants, and a good one. Springtime is definitely asparagus time at the Berlin, but all year long you can order up schnitzels, goulash, sauerbraten, and all those other Teutonic temptations. The lunch menu also offers up soups, salads, and sandwiches. Open Monday through Thursday 11:00 A.M. to 10:00 P.M., Friday and Saturday 11:00 A.M. to 11:00 P.M., and Sunday 4:00 to 10:00 P.M. Moderate. Metro stop: Union Station (red line).

Il Radicchio, 223 Pennsylvania Avenue SE; 547–5114. One of a chain of four reasonably priced trattorias around the District run by one of Washington top restaurateurs. The rules are simple: all the spaghetti you can eat for $6.50 and you pay extra for each helping of one of the twenty sauces available. Also thick

Where to Find the Author's Favorite Places to Eat in Capitol Hill and Northeast

Union Station
Forty restaurants and cafes within Union Station
(see page 39 for full listing)

Dubliner Pub
520 North Capitol Street; 737–3773
(see page 39 for full listing)

Kelly's Irish Times
14th and F Streets; 543–5433
(see page 39 for full listing)

The Market Lunch
Located at the Eastern Market
(see page 47 for full listing)

Tunnicliff's
222 Seventh Street SE; 546–3663
(see page 48 for full listing)

Bluestone Cafe
327 Seventh Street SE; 547–9007
(see page 49 for full listing)

Bread and Chocolate
666 Pennsylvania Avenue SE; 547–2875
(see page 49 for full listing)

Cup of Dreams
2639 Twelfth Street NE; 526–6562
(see page 51 for full listing)

The Monocle
107 D Street NE; 546–4488
(see page 53 for full listing)

La Colline
400 North Capitol Street NW; 737–0400
(see page 53 for full listing)

Italian panini and great pizza. No reservations. Open Monday through Thursday 11:30 A.M. to 10:00 P.M., until 11:00 on Friday and Saturday. Inexpensive. Metro stop: Capitol South (orange and blue lines).

Two Quail, 320 Massachusetts Avenue NE; 543–8030. Local restaurant critics invariably rank Two Quail among Washington's most romantic restaurants because of its comfy, hidden corners and eclectic, intensively decorated surroundings. The menu is also eclectic, ranging from Pad Thai to Muscovy duck and, yes, stuffed quail (with bacon and cheese). Reservations essential. Moderate. Metro stop: Union Station (red line).

The Waterfront and Anacostia

Washington owes its very existence and its role as our capital to its riverfront location at the head of navigation on the Potomac, at the point where it meets the Anacostia River. In selecting this site, George Washington hoped that the new capital, then a Maryland swamp "on the easterly bank of the Potomac," would be one of the young republic's major deepwater ports, a transfer point between ocean transport and the planned canal system that led back into Ohio and other frontier regions. Although the Seventh Street wharf, the current site of the Washington Marina, was one of the country's busiest ports in antebellum days and the Washington Navy Yard occupied an important role in the life of the city until well into the nineteenth century, Washington's long riverfront has slipped into disuse. That said, the banks of the Anacostia and the Potomac have some terrific opportunities for anyone exploring off-the-beaten-path Washington. What they do not offer, however, is a wide selection of places to stay.

Start your waterfront experience by taking the Metro to the L'Enfant Plaza stop (all lines except red) and walk 4 blocks to the *Maine Avenue Fish Market,* located well off the beaten path on the Potomac's Washington Channel in the shadow of the 14th Street bridge. Here you'll stroll into an open-air, high-protein scene to find the bounty of the Chesapeake spread out before you on barges, where aproned vendors preside over rows of glistening, freshly caught rockfish, catfish, bluefish, and carp. And since we're talking Chesapeake Bay, there are bushel baskets crammed with oysters and that Eastern Shore delicacy, blue crab. Open daily 7:30 A.M. to 8:00 P.M., the market draws a large number of customers searching for finny friends from other lands and a cadre of chefs from local Asian restaurants.

If all of this triggers a hunger pang or two, no problem. You'll find a number of possibilities for highly informal dining in the market at places like *Captain White's,* where a seafood combo of oysters, shrimp, scallops, and fish tops the bill, and *Jessie Taylor Seafood* for steamed crab legs and shrimp, plus a nifty raw bar. Both are open from 8:00 A.M. to 9:00 P.M. Another option is *Custis and Brown,* open 10:30 A.M. to

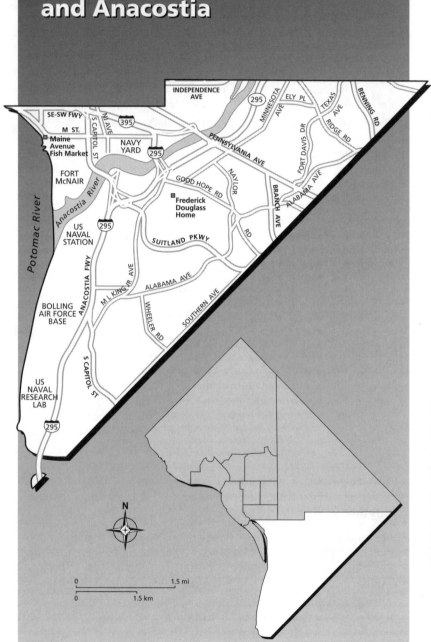

The Waterfront and Anacostia

THE WATERFRONT AND ANACOSTIA

TOP ATTRACTIONS IN
THE WATERFRONT AND ANACOSTIA

Maine Avenue Fish Market

Arena Stage

Washington Navy Yard

Navy Museum

Marine Museum

Marine Barracks

Cedar Hill

7:00 P.M., which modestly advertises "The Best Hot Cooked Crabs in Town."

You can explore the waterfront area very nicely and have a picnic in the process by picking up some Fish Market take-out and following the riverside promenade that begins behind Le Rivage and runs along the Washington Marina for several blocks. As you'll learn, the riverside walk is a favorite with fishermen and sightseers who enjoy the views across the Potomac to Hains Point Park and its municipal golf course and, beyond that, the shores of Virginia and Arlington Cemetery. Your stroll will also take you past some of the many luxury powerboats and sailboats that anchor there regularly and a colony of elaborate houseboats, where a number of lucky Washingtonians enjoy life on a permanent cruise on the Potomac.

When you reach Sixth Street, the round (polygonal, actually) building on the left is the **Arena Stage,** a multitheater complex that enjoys a massive local and national reputation for the quality of its productions and of its resident theater company. Of the Arena's three stages, the 827-seat Fichandler (named for one of the Arena's 1950 cofounders), reflects the Arena's origins as theater-in-the-round. Its neighbor, the Kreeger Theatre, which seats 500, is fan-shaped, and the more intimate Old Vat is configured for cabaret. All three serve up a rich schedule that includes contemporary plays, experimental works, and even some musicals. Call 488–3300 or consult either the *Washington Post* or *City Paper* to see what's playing when you're in town. The Arena Stage complex is located at Sixth Street and Maine Avenue SW. Parking is available. Metro: Waterfront (green line).

Also to the left, in a charming park vibrant with azaleas, is one of Washington's oldest structures, the **Thomas Law House,** built in 1796 by a wealthy, eccentric land speculator who married into Washington and American nobility when he wed Eliza Custis, Martha Washington's granddaughter. This marriage was not made in heaven, and it ended in 1804 with Washington's first power divorce, but that didn't keep the miserable couple from having President John Adams and King Louis Philippe of France over for dinner in their splendid Federal mansion. Today Eliza would probably cringe at learning that her Washington home is *(a)* named after her disagreeable husband and *(b)* also known as the "Honeymoon Cottage." The Law House is located at 461 North Street SW

OFF THE BEATEN PATH

Capital Quote

"It is very unhealthy. Few people would live in Washington who were not obliged to reside there."

—American Notes, *1842*

and is not generally open to the public. For an appointment to visit the house and its selection of period antiques, call 554–4844 between 9:00 A.M. and 5:00 P.M. Monday through Friday.

The riverside walk will take you past the piers at Sixth and Water Streets, home port to a pair of the District's leading dinner and sightseeing cruise lines.

Spirit Cruises operates the *Potomac Spirit* and the *Spirit of Washington* on lunch and dinner cruises featuring live entertainment, ample buffets, dancing, and a chance to see the District's waterfront and landmarks from an entirely new angle. The company also offers special cruises downriver to visit Mt. Vernon. For schedules and prices, call 554–8000 or visit www.spiritofwashington.com.

Odyssey Cruises operates *Odyssey III,* a mammoth version of the glassed-in *bateaux mouches* that take visitors to Paris up and down the Seine. Dancing and live music, plus lunch, dinner, and a Sunday jazz brunch. And for all of you romantics, there's also a moonlight cruise available. Call 488–6000 or visit www.odysseycruises.com.

After passing the docks you'll see the **Titanic Memorial,** an impressive but politically incorrect statue dedicated to the gentlemen who lost their lives by giving up their lifeboat seats to the ladies in that 1912 disaster.

A left turn leads to the entrance of **Fort Leslie J. McNair,** strategically located on the Potomac to defend the city, which is why it was part of L'Enfant's original plan and one of Washington's first military bases when it opened in 1791 as an arsenal; it is also one of the most beautiful locations in the city. Despite all that fancy strategic planning, the British had no trouble torching the arsenal during their occupation of Washington in 1814, and Fort McNair has gone through many renovations ever since. Today its broad lawns and Beaux Arts buildings are best known as the site of the **National War College,** where military and foreign affairs leaders, in a one-year sabbatical, take courses to improve their professional skills and take a fresh look at their world and its culture.

Fort McNair is a great place to stroll along the river past "Generals Row," the white-columned officers' houses that conjure up memories of those Hollywood frontier forts with their broad parade grounds and tidy military housing. Over by the tennis courts, at the north end of the fort, you'll find a historical marker recording that four of the Lincoln conspirators were hanged on that spot in July 1865. The building next to the courts is all that remains of the 1826 Federal Penitentiary, where the plotters were held until their execution. Fort Mc Nair is located at 103 Third Street SW. Presentation of a photo ID is usually enough to get you into the fort during daylight hours; during periods of heightened security concerns, however, admission can be difficult. Better call 685–3196 first or ask the MPs at the gate.

Once America's largest shipyard, the **Washington Navy Yard,** which dates back to America's earliest days, was burned to prevent its falling into British hands during the War of 1812. Rebuilt in classic Victorian red brick, the yard is now the home of two terrific military museums. The Navy Yard is located at 901 M Street SE. Metro: The yard is a twenty-minute walk from the Eastern Market station (orange and blue lines). Parking is available. You'll need to show a picture ID at the main gate. Call 433–4882.

Once inside, head for the **Navy Museum,** in the old Naval Gun Factory, which covers every aspect of U.S. naval history, from the Revolution right down to Vietnam. Exhibits range from the gun deck from "Old Ironsides" to a replica of Admiral Byrd's hut from the Antarctic Expedition of 1933. The museum's vast collection of hands-on World War II exhibits includes film shows, electronic reconstructions of key naval battles, and nostalgic displays of life on the 1942 home front. Even though they might never have seen John Wayne save democracy, visitors can tour the destroyer *Barry,* another artifact of World War II, which is permanently anchored nearby. Or you could experience life on a submarine, with operating periscopes so kids can track enemy carriers to their hearts' content. The Navy Museum, in building 76, is open Monday through Friday 9:00 A.M. to 4:00 P.M. (until 5:00 P.M. April through September), Saturday and Sunday 10:00 A.M. to 5:00 P.M. Call 433–4882.

The yard's **Marine Museum,** also housed in a Victorian-era factory building, uses a "time tunnel" of uniforms, weapons, and battle memorabilia to guide visitors chronologically through the Corps' glorious history. Dioramas show scenes from some of the Marines' most gallant and critical battles in World Wars I and II, Korea, and Vietnam, along with an explanation of the strategies and tactics behind each engagement. One high point: the collection of Marine treasures that includes the famous flag raised on Mt. Suribachi on Iwo Jima. The Marine Museum is located in building 58 and is open Monday through Saturday 10:00 A.M. to 4:00 P.M., Sunday noon to 5:00 P.M. Call 433–3534.

The Navy Yard is a rich oasis of military history located in a restaurant desert, but you won't need to call in the Marines to fight hunger. You'll find William III, an upscale deli with thick sandwiches in building 36 near the Marine Museum, open 6:30 A.M. to 2:30 P.M. If you want a more elaborate lunch, head for the former Officer's Club in building 101 (11:00 A.M. to 1:30 P.M.), and if fast food will do, Mc Donald's, in building 184, is open 5:00 A.M. to 5:00 P.M.

The **Marine Barracks,** located at Eighth and I Streets, were built in 1801 on a site personally selected by President Thomas Jefferson because of its strategic defensive situation between the Navy Yard and the Capitol. Although its military significance has long vanished, this massive, walled quadrangle—"The Oldest Post of the Corps"—remains the epicenter of Marine tradition and spectacle. This is the home of the Marine Commandant, who lives in an 1805 house on the Parade Ground and the ground zero of Marine history. It is also the headquarters of the Marine Band, which will always be identified with its legendary leader, the world's "March King," John Philip Sousa.

Anacostia Farmer's Market
If you're in Anacostia and hankering for fresh produce, the Anacostia Farmer's Market convenes every Friday between June and November in the parking lot of the Union Temple Baptist Church, 1225 W Street SE, Hours: 4:00 to 6:30 P.M.

Well before Sousa's day, its perfectly manicured Parade Ground was the scene of the Corps' most hallowed rituals. You'll definitely want to see the most stirring of those ceremonies, the Friday Evening Parade, an inspiring patriotic pageant with precision drills, brilliant uniforms, flashing sabers, martial fanfares, and enough Sousa marches to set the most ardent pacifist ablaze. Speaking of the March King, Sousa Hall, which looks across the Parade Ground at the Commandant's House, is the sanctum sanctorum for the legions of Sousaphiles throughout the world. Here, at the headquarters of the Marine Band, you'll see a wealth of Sousiana, including a library of his original sheet music, personal mementos, and a large hall where today's band members practice under a large portrait of Sousa himself.

Guided tours of the barracks leave regularly from the main gate at Eighth and I Streets between 8:00 A.M. and 4:00 P.M. daily; all you need to do is turn up. Admission to Sousa Hall is also possible, but because of the regular morning Marine Band practice, tours are usually possible only between noon and 4:00 P.M. For information about this and the Friday evening parade, call 433–6060. The parade is given only from

May through August and starts at 8:45 P.M. Reservations for the parade require written requests well in advance, by writing to: Protocol Office, Attn.: Parades, Marine Barracks, Eighth and T Streets SE, Washington, D.C. 20390-5000. Your request should include the names of the people in your party, your return address, and a point of contact with a telephone number; you should also specify an alternate parade date in case your preferred date is unavailable. That said, you'll stand an excellent chance of getting in by joining the general admission line, which forms at the main gate on Friday evenings, but since seating is first come first served, plan to arrive before 8:00 P.M. The barracks has a nifty Web site at www.mbw.usmc.mil.

An eclectic group from every era of American history is buried in the *Congressional Cemetery,* a quiet corner of the capital where American notables have been interred since 1807. The cemetery is the final resting place of military leaders of all wars since the Revolution, as well as Declaration of Independence signer Elbridge Gerry, Pushmataha (the son of Apache chief Cochise), and Civil War leaders from both sides. Many of the cemetery's Congressional guests are buried under peculiar, mushroomlike monuments that prompted one U.S. senator to comment that "the prospect of being interred under these atrocities brings a new terror to death."

After the John Philip Sousa plot, the cemetery's most visited graves include those of Lincoln photographer Mathew Brady, J. Edgar Hoover, and Belva Lockwood, the first woman to run for President. And every November 6, Sousa's birthday, the Marine Band visits his grave to lay a wreath and play his marches in musical tribute to its former leader. A self-guided tour brochure is available at the office. The Congressional Cemetery, at 1801 E Street SE (543–0539), is open daily from dawn to dusk. Metro: Stadium-Armory (orange and blue lines).

Across the Anacostia River from the Navy Yard is the section known as Anacostia. Because of its crime rate, out-of-town visitors should exercise caution, especially at night. Its historic significance, however, makes the area worth a visit. An early guidebook called Anacostia "the eastern slice of Washington . . . a place that developed slowly and independently." Because of its physical separation by the river from the rest of the District, Anacostia from its earliest days had a life of its own, starting as a collection of stand-alone villages within the District. Today's Anacostia is an almost entirely African-American residential and commercial community, but in the nineteenth century, Anacostia brought together residents of many backgrounds in settlements like

Furniture Frenzy

*I*f you'd like to do some megashopping, even if it's just the window variety, or if you're looking for some decorating ideas, stop off at one of the East's top design showcases, the **Washington Design Center,** which brings together dozens of major manufacturers of furniture, textiles, and kitchen and bath equipment under one roof.

Although this sumptuous collection is aimed at designers and the trade, the public is welcome in many, but not all, showrooms from 9:00 A.M. to 5:00 P.M. Monday through Thursday and from 10:00 A.M. to 3:00 P.M. on Saturday. Purchases, however, can be made only by design professionals.

Having said that, if you've found something you absolutely must have, you can get it by hiring a designer on the spot. The center's front desk will help you find one ASAP. Washington Design Center, 300 D Street SW. Call 646–6101. Metro: Federal Center (orange and blue lines).

Uniontown, a mainly white community, Stantontown, where free blacks lived, and other villages where German immigrants prevailed.

On a knoll in Anacostia stands *Cedar Hill,* the Victorian frame home of African-American leader Frederick Douglass. Born a slave in 1818, Douglass, after teaching himself to read and write, became a publisher, bank president, diplomat, musician, fiery orator, and the author of hundreds of books, monographs, and speeches; he somehow also found time to learn seven languages and serve as the American Minister to Haiti. This Renaissance man's greatest achievements, however, were in the political arena as an eloquent advocate of abolition, women's rights, and racial justice, and as a trusted adviser to Abraham Lincoln on these issues.

Visitors to Cedar Hill wander through rooms filled with mementos of Douglass's extraordinary life, including his beloved Stradivarius, Abraham Lincoln's cane (a gift from Mary Lincoln), and a leather rocking chair given to Douglass by a grateful Haitian people. The dining room stands ready for one of the formal dinners Douglass gave for fellow members of the Washington power grid of the 1880s, while his library bursts with more than 1,100 books and a massive rolltop desk covered with papers. A visit to Cedar Hill will also give you a spectacular hilltop panorama of the Capitol and other Washington landmarks. Cedar Hill is located at 1411 W Street SE. The House and its adjoining National Park Visitor Center, where you can view a film of Douglass's life, are open from 9:00 A.M. to 5:00 P.M. in the summer, until 4:00 P.M. the rest of the year. Tours are scheduled throughout the day, but call (800) 365–2267 for the latest schedule. Tour fees: $3.00 for adults, $1.50 for seniors, under six free. No Metro.

Another showcase of African-American history and culture is the **Anacostia Museum and Center,** located in a former school at 1901 Fort Place SE. The Anacostia Museum will be closed for renovation until mid-2001. When it reopens, you'll see one of Washington's liveliest and most thoughtful collections and exhibits of African-American art and history. The museum's phone number is 287–3369; you can keep in touch about the exact date of reopening and new operating hours by calling the Smithsonian information line, which is 357–2700. No Metro or bus stops.

PLACES TO EAT IN
THE WATERFRONT AND
ANACOSTIA

Le Rivage, 1000 Water Street SW; 488-8111. The seafood speaks with a French accent and specialties include the *moules* (mussels), great lobster, grilled fish, and crab-stuffed chicken. Open for lunch Monday through Friday 11:30 A.M. to 2:00 P.M. and for dinner Monday through Thursday 5:30 to 10:30 P.M., Friday and Saturday 5:30 to11:00 P.M., Sunday 5:00 to 9:00 P.M. Moderate.

Phillips Flagship, 900 Water Street SW; 488-8515. Takes the self-serve approach, with huge seafood buffets at reasonable prices. Phillips is pop-ular with tour groups, especially for Sunday brunch, which is practically overwhelming. Open Monday through Thursday 11:00 A.M. to 11:00 P.M., Friday 11:00 A.M. to midnight, Saturday noon to midnight, and Sunday 10:30 A.M. to 10:00 P.M. Moderate.

Hogate's, 800 Water Street SW; 484-6300. You'll also have lots of company and a megacalorie experience at this Washington landmark that prides itself on its crab cakes, lobster, and clambakes. Open Monday through Thursday 11:00 A.M. to 11:00 P.M., Friday 11:00 A.M. to midnight, Saturday noon to midnight, and Sunday 10:30 A.M. to 10:00 P.M. Moderate.

Where to Find the Author's Favorite Places to Eat in the Waterfront and Anacostia

Captain White's
Located at the Maine Avenue Fish Market
(see page 59 for full listing)

Jessie Taylor Seafood
Located at the Maine Avenue Fish Market
(see page 59 for full listing)

Custis and Brown
Located at the Maine Avenue Fish Market
(see page 59 for full listing)

Foggy Bottom

Although Foggy Bottom is the home of the State Department, it did not get its name from the torrents of bafflegab and diplo-speak that gush forth daily from America's Foreign Policy Headquarters, known locally as "the fudge factory." This neighborhood was originally named Funkstown for Jacob Funk, the German immigrant who founded a small industrial community on the Potomac that clearly would have trouble meeting today's pollution standards. In addition to scads of smoke and pollutants, Herr Funk's riverfront slum also suffered from the gases and other emanations of its surrounding swamps, adding up to a perpetual haze that gave this OSHA paradise its picturesque name. That said, the State Department hasn't helped much.

Today's Foggy Bottom gives new meaning to the term "mixed use." Its tenants include large government agencies, embassies, the Watergate, the Daughters of the American Revolution and major institutions such as the grandiose Kennedy Center and sprawling George Washington University, along with more human-scale neighborhoods where narrow nineteenth-century row houses line leafy residential streets.

In fact, a good place to start a visit to Foggy Bottom is at its most elegant home. *The Octagon,* known in its day as "The Palace of Washington," must have seemed wildly out of place among the crude shacks and muddy streets of the young capital. Built by Col. John Tayloe in 1801, this grand Federal town house was designed by William Thornton, the architect of the U.S. Capitol. Jefferson, Monroe, Adams, and Andrew Jackson all passed through the Octagon's circular entrance hall to visit the Tayloes in their splendid home. The Octagon added an entirely new and unwelcome chapter to its history when for six months it served as the Executive Mansion for President Madison after the British burned the White House during the War of 1812. After a long period of decay as a tenement, the Octagon was rescued and restored in 1902 by the American Institute of Architects, which still maintains it as the oldest museum in the United States devoted to architecture.

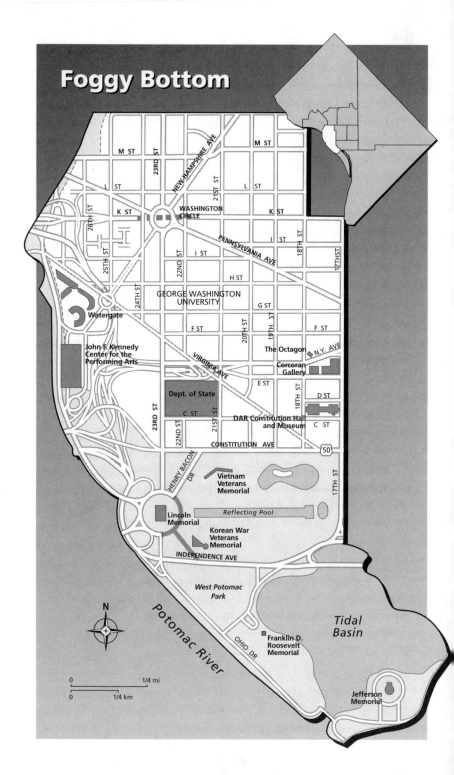

Foggy Bottom

The Octagon

Your guided tour will start in the drawing room, once covered with 4 feet of trash, where you'll see the priceless stone mantel that somehow survived those years of neglect. You'll pass through the dining room, with its Chippendale breakfront and Gilbert Stuart portraits of the Tayloes, before climbing the splendid oval staircase. Check out the ivory "amity buttons" on the handrail, which indicated that the house was paid for, an early American custom that few could follow today. Upstairs in the oval study stands the English rent table where Madison signed the Treaty of Ghent, which ended the war with Great Britain. The house's bedrooms, which are regularly occupied by traveling historical and architectural exhibits, are reportedly haunted by the ghosts of two Tayloe daughters who threw themselves down the staircase when told by their father they could not marry the men of their choice. Odd noises, swaying chandeliers, and mysterious footsteps are not included in the tour.

Down in the basement where President Madison stashed the presidential wine and servants toiled in the large kitchen, this magnificent home shows its human side. The restored "servant's hall" is where the Tayloe's African-American servants ate and did their household chores, then slept in shifts under impossibly cramped conditions in the small bedroom next door. As you'll see from drawings and cross sections, extensive archaeological research and reconstruction have restored all the original walls and structures of the basement rooms.

The Octagon, 1799 New York Avenue NW (638–3221) is open Tuesday through Sunday 10:00 A.M. to 4:00 P.M.; closed Mondays. Admission is $5.00 for adults, $3.00 for students and seniors. Metro: Farragut West and McPherson Square (orange and blue lines) or Farragut North (red line).

The headquarters building of the **American Institute of Architects,** at 1735 New York Avenue, behind the Octagon, offers regular architectural exhibits in its lobby. The building and its shop, which carries a broad selection of books on architecture, are open Monday through Friday 8:30 A.M. to 5:00 P.M.

Although the **Corcoran Gallery of Art** is on a lot of people's "must-see" lists, it's also slightly off the beaten path because it's *(a)* off the Mall, *(b)* generally not as well known as the more publicized National Gallery of Art, and *(c)* one of the few great Washington museums not part of the Smithsonian family. The Corcoran Collection moved to its splendid Beaux Arts building in 1897, when it outgrew what is now the Renwick Gallery. Before entering, take a look at the imposing rotunda and the facade frieze bearing the names of great painters and you'll see why the Corcoran was Frank Lloyd Wright's favorite building in Washington.

Inside you'll find a large, distinguished, and eclectic permanent collection of classic and contemporary American and European art. Here the luminous work of French impressionists mingles with American works such as Albert Bierstadt's epic *The Last of the Buffalo,* the famous Gilbert Stuart portrait of George Washington seen on the $1.00 bill and even a thirteenth-century stained glass window from Soissons Cathedral. Although the Corcoran's famous statue *The Greek Slave* scandalized Victorian-era visitors, who gazed on it in gender-segregated viewings, nobody gives it a thought today, especially anyone who's been to the movies since 1970. The Museum also has numerous special exhibits of contemporary American art and photography.

Our last visit occurred during one of the museum's periodic "family days," which featured performances of Colonial music and dance, children's art lessons, and "appearances" by Abraham Lincoln and a crinkly Benjamin Franklin, who told stories to the kids. The museum shop, well-stocked with art and photography books, is a real treat. So is the Cafe Des Artistes in the museum's double atrium, which offers light fare Wednesday to Monday 11:00 A.M. to 2:00 P.M., until 8:00 on Thursday; closed Tuesday. There's a Cajun-influenced gospel brunch every Sunday

11:00 A.M. to 2:00 P.M. Every Wednesday 12:30 to 1:30 P.M. a free program of live jazz is presented in the museum's Hammer Auditorium.

The Corcoran, at 500 17th Street NW (639–1700, www.corcoran.org), is open daily 10:00 A.M. to 5:00 P.M. except Tuesday, until 9:00 P.M. on Thursday. Docents lead forty-five-minute tours at noon on weekdays, and on weekends at 10:30 A.M., noon, and 2:30 P.M. Suggested donations: $5.00 for families, $3.00 for individuals, and $1.00 for seniors and students. Metro: Farragut West (orange and blue lines).

The block-square *Daughters of the American Revolution* (DAR) complex includes a museum, a genealogical reference library, and a series of richly furnished rooms depicting typical upscale American rooms during the period 1770–1840. It also includes one of the city's finest auditoriums, the 4,000 seat Constitution Hall. The DAR may have a fusty image in some areas, but its museum comes up with snazzy displays of American decorative art, most recently an exhibit of colorful and intricately made quilts from Colonial times right down to the present. A collection of early American ceramics includes useful medical equipment such as a handsome leech jar to hold the friendly little critters that will happily cleanse that pesky bile from your blood, and you know how important that can be. After all, if it was good enough for (the late) George Washington, it's good enough for you.

Docents also take visitors to the DAR's "period rooms" on tours that depart every forty-five minutes. Among the standouts are the New Jersey Room, with walls paneled in walnut retrieved from a ship that sank

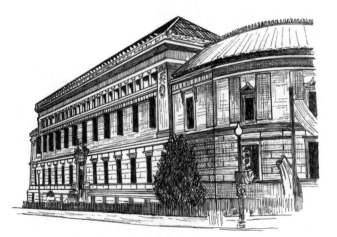

Corcoran Gallery of Art

Memorial Walk

*T*he best way to see the off-the-beaten-path Franklin Delano Roosevelt Memorial and four other important memorials is by taking a half-day stroll that meanders across the National Mall, through the park and polo fields along the Potomac, and winds up at the Jefferson Memorial for a look at the cherry trees around the Tidal Basin.

From the Foggy Bottom Metro exit, turn right on 23rd Street and walk past the State Department to Constitution Avenue, where a left turn takes you to the most poignant spot in Washington, the **Vietnam Veteran's Memorial**, with its wall of black granite bearing the names of the 58,000 Americans who died in that war. Offerings, flowers, and mementos of the fallen are often left at the wall and the emotions of their surviving buddies, relatives, and ordinary visitors are always close to the surface.

At the **Lincoln Memorial** at the end of the National Mall, the magnificent Daniel Chester French statue symbolizes Lincoln's greatness. But this memorial is loaded with other symbolic touches. The thirty-six exterior Doric columns represent the number of states in the Union when Lincoln was shot, while the fifty-six steps up to the statue mark Lincoln's age at the time of his death. Then take a close look at Lincoln's hands; one is clenched and the other open, which reputedly represents both his will to preserve the Union and act with openness and compassion. Probably so, but they are also signing his initials, **A** with the left and **L** with the right.

To the right of the Lincoln Memorial you'll pass the **Korean War Veterans Memorial**, which honors the fighting men and women who served in one of America's bloodiest and most frustrating conflicts. The memorial's centerpiece is the group of nineteen stainless steel statues depicting a squad on patrol and the images on black granite of more than 2,400 servicemen and -women.

Signs will direct you across Independence Avenue to Ohio Drive and a walk along the Potomac through West Potomac Park, past soccer fields, baseball diamonds, and even Washington's only polo fields.

At the **Franklin Delano Roosevelt Memorial** you'll walk through four granite-walled spaces, one for each of Roosevelt's four administrations. On the walls are inscribed memorable phrases from FDR's speeches; sculptures dramatize the challenges Roosevelt and other Americans faced in each of his terms. In the first room, haggard and hungry men stand in a Depression breadline for handouts; in another sculpture, a man listens to a radio for inspiration from one of Roosevelt's "fireside chats." In the third room the wartime president sits with his dog Fala and in the fourth, a statue of Eleanor Roosevelt commemorates her role as First Lady and champion of human rights.

Exiting the FDR Memorial you'll be next to the Tidal Basin and ready to continue your stroll among the cherry trees to the **Jefferson Memorial,** a few yards away. Then head for the Smithsonian Metro stop and your next off-the-beaten-path destination.

FOGGY BOTTOM

AUTHOR'S FAVORITES IN FOGGY BOTTOM

State Department Diplomatic Reception Rooms

Corcoran Gallery

Octagon

Franklin Delano Roosevelt Memorial

Vietnam Veteran's Memorial

in 1777, the California Room, which faithfully reproduces a room of the whaling station in Monterey as it appeared in the early 1800s, and a Maryland Room with wallpaper depicting Baltimore in 1770 that was discovered in a Paris antique shop by a DAR member.

If you're interested in tracing your Colonial-era ancestors, the DAR's vast genealogical library, located in Continental Hall, the building's elaborate theater, is one of the best research sources anywhere. A $5.00 fee will start you off with one of the in-house professional genealogists and a computer to track down your family.

The DAR also offers a "Colonial Adventure" tour; Costumed guides take five- to seven-year-olds on a travel in time back to Colonial America, where they play eighteenth-century games, attend a period tea party, and learn what it was like to be a child in pre-Revolutionary days.

The Daughters of the American Revolution Museum, 1776 D Street NW (879–3241, www. dar.org/museum), is open Monday through Friday 8:30 A.M. to 4:00 P.M., Sunday 1:00 to 5:00 P.M.; closed Saturday. Tours of the period rooms are offered Monday through Friday 10:30 A.M. to 2:30 P.M. and Sunday 1:00 to 4:00 P.M. The genealogical library is open Monday through Friday 9:00 A.M. to 5:00 P.M. and Sunday 1:00 to 5:00 P.M. "Colonial Adventure" tours are given the second and fourth Sunday of every month from 1:30 to 2:30 P.M. and from 3:00 to 4:00 P.M. Admission is free, but reservations are essential and, because of the tour's popularity, should be made early.

Capital Quote

"Diplomacy is the art of saying 'nice doggie' until you can find a rock or a tree."

—*Will Rogers*

The *Art Museum of the Americas,* which occupies a charming Spanish colonial building behind its parent organization, the Organization of American States, showcases contemporary art of Latin America and the Caribbean. At the museum you'll always find exhibits of vibrant works from its extensive permanent collection, probably accompanied by at least one temporary exhibit presenting an established or emerging artist from somewhere in the hemisphere. Although the art is always special, be sure to see the fascinating loggia in the back of the museum, where two stories of blue and terra-cotta tiles replicate Aztec figures, legends, and folk themes. Art Museum of the Americas, 201 18th Street NW (458–6301, fax 458–6021, www.oas.org/museum), is open Tuesday through Sunday

Funky Bottom

Jacob Funk and Funkstown may be ancient history, but their Zeitgeist lives on at Foggy Bottom's United Church, at 1920 G Street NW, which regularly offers services in German.

10:00 A.M. to 5:00 P.M. Donations suggested. Metro: Farragut West (blue and orange lines).

Although it looks pretty dull from the street, behind its New Deal Modern facade, the Department of the Interior offers visitors a pair of unique places. Exhibits in the *Department of the Interior Museum,* trace the Department's main areas of activity, which include the protection of wildlife, mine safety, and western lands. The real crowd pleasers, however, are the colorful Bureau of Indian Affairs exhibits of Native American culture, crafts, and heritage. If you're impressed by the exhibits, across the hall there's an authentic off-the-beaten-path find: The *Indian Craft Shop,* one of Washington's top gift shops, has a nifty collection of woven goods, pottery, and jewelry from forty-five tribal groups. The intricate Alaskan carvings from walrus ivory are in themselves worth a visit. The Department of the Interior Museum (208–4743, www.doi.gov/museum/intmu1) and its Craft Shop (208–4056) at 1849 C Street NW, are open Monday through Friday 8:30 A.M. to 4:30 P.M. Photo ID required for entry. Metro: Farragut West (orange and blue lines).

Let's be clear—when you take the weekly tour of the *Federal Reserve Bank,* Alan Greenspan is not going to come out to brief you personally about his innermost thoughts on interest rates or the direction of the stock market. What you will get is a well-organized tour of one of America's and the world's most powerful institutions, which directly influences the health of the economy and interest rates (important only if you're one of the few with a car loan, mortgage, or credit card). You can sample the

All About GWU

*G*eorge Washington University originated in the dream of both Washington and L'Enfant to establish a national university in the District somewhere near the current intersection of 23rd Street and Virginia Avenue. Washington, in fact, held stock in the Potowmack Canal Company, which was founded to create both the university and the C&O Canal. Long story short, Congress never voted to create a national school, but the idea morphed into Columbian College, founded in 1824, which became today's GWU. After the federal government, the university is the largest single private landholder in the city and growing every year.

FOGGY BOTTOM

rarefied air of the Fed's headquarters, with its templelike pillared entrance hall, by visiting the Federal Reserve Board Gallery, a tasteful exhibit of nineteenth- and twentieth-century paintings and sculpture; a recent show featured imaginative sculptures and sketches based on banknotes.

But for a complete look at America's cathedral of cash, take the weekly tour, which visits the gallery, then ascends the graceful stairway to the holiest of holies, the huge Board of Governor's Boardroom. Here, around a 27-foot, two-ton granite table, the world's most influential banker and his colleagues make big decisions that affect you. In fact, you can watch the excellent film describing the Fed's workings from Greenspan's chair and think about getting that mortgage paid off. As a souvenir of your visit, your guide will even give you some money, a little bag of shredded cash. (Here's a tip for parents: If the kids are getting fidgety or bored, you can keep them amused for a decade or two by asking them to reassemble the bills). And, oh yes, there's a pay phone outside where you can call your broker. The Federal Reserve Bank, at 20th and C Streets, offers building tours from the C Street entrance every Thursday at 2:30 P.M. Call the Visitor Office at 452–3149 for information. The gallery is open Tuesday through Friday from 11:30 A.M. to 2:30 P.M. You can join Alan and his merry men in the boardroom at one of the six to eight board meetings that are open to the public each year; call 452–3206 to see if one's being held when you're in town.

Someone (I think it was me) once described the huge **Department of State building** at 22nd and C Streets NW as "a '50s insurance office without the charm." You definitely wouldn't want to tour the rabbit warren offices on the first six floors, and even if you could visit the rarefied seventh floor (which you can't), you'd find that even the secretary of state's suite suffers from the klunky boardroom decor so cherished on Planet Eisenhower.

But the eighth floor **Diplomatic Reception Rooms** are a very different story. Here you'll find an unparalleled collection of eighteenth-century American furniture, paintings, and decorative arts that is one of the city's best-kept secrets. The world leaders, foreign diplomats, and other dignitaries that attend receptions and dinners in these opulent rooms wine and dine surrounded by treasures such as Thomas Jefferson's mahogany desk, where he wrote portions of the Declaration of Independence; the

Namesake

secretary on which the Treaty of Paris was signed in 1783, ending the American Revolution; and a large collection of Philadelphia Chippendale chairs. Portraits of John Jay and the Washingtons by Gilbert Stuart look down from the walls, while George Washington's dinner service is displayed in a massive breakfront. The secretary of state's intimate dinners for 250 are held in the vast Franklin dining room, where the carpet is so large that it had to be helicoptered in.

Forty-five minute guided tours of the Reception Rooms are conducted Monday through Friday at 9:30 and 10:30 A.M., and 2:45 P.M. and leave from the flag-filled lobby you've seen on every network TV news show. No admission charge, but reservations are required; get them by calling 647–3241 or faxing 736–4232. Summer tours are fully booked up to three months in advance, so you must plan ahead. Children under twelve discouraged. Metro: Foggy Bottom (orange and blue lines).

You don't have to be a rocket scientist to appreciate the **National Academy of Sciences** headquarters building at 2100 C Street NW. The Academy's stunning Great Hall, with a four-story ceiling of gold and blue mosaics depicting great moments in the history of science, is similar in form and appearance to a small medieval church. A Foucault pendulum, which illustrates spinning of the earth on its axis, dangles from the center of the dome. The hall and its surrounding corridors usually house small art shows; free chamber music concerts are frequently given under the "Arts in the Academy" program.

Downstairs, the Academy's small, health-conscious cafeteria makes a good lunch stop. Afterward, head for the building's gardens on Constitution Avenue, where you'll find a giant bronze statue of the great scientist Albert Einstein. A celestial map, showing the heavens as they were on April 22, 1979, the day the memorial was dedicated, is spread at Einstein's feet. In his left hand is a paper with mathematical equations that summarize his most important contributions: the theory of relativity, the photoelectric effect, and the equivalence of energy and matter. To round out your visit, offer to explain all three to your spouse and children. The Academy (334–2000) is open Monday through Friday 8:30 A.M. to 5:00 P.M. The cafeteria is open 7:00 to 10:30 A.M. and to visitors for lunch from 12:45 to 2:00 P.M. For information on concerts, call 334–2436. Metro: Foggy Bottom (orange and blue lines).

Watergate, where a botched break-in of Democratic party headquarters triggered the investigation and cover-up that led to Nixon's resignation and added a new word to our language, takes its name from the tiers of granite steps still visible along the Potomac just to the north of Memorial Bridge. The steps were originally envisioned as a ceremonial "water gate" where foreign dignitaries would arrive by barge, Cleopatra-like, for a formal welcome to the capital. It never happened. Instead, Washingtonians gathered here on the steps or in canoes for summer evening concerts by the Marine Band and other orchestras playing on a bandshell anchored on the river.

The apartment-office-hotel complex, which resembles a Mussolini-era Italian luxury liner that has mysteriously run aground on the banks of the Potomac, later gave part of its name to the continuing and unfortunate habit of making every minor scandal or passing illegality a "gate" of some kind. But another, real Watergate scandal came along during the '90s when it was the address of Ms. Lewinsky; the apartments are also home to Monica's neighbors, presidential candidates Robert and Elizabeth Dole.

The office building where Tricky Dick's "plumbers" broke in is at 2500 Virginia Avenue, while the Howard Johnson across the street that was used by their lookouts is now a George Washington University dorm. Behind the office building, the posh Swisshotel Watergate Hotel contains Aquarelle—an equally pricey restaurant—and a mediocre health club. If hunger strikes in this virtually restaurant-free zone, you could get a loan and head for Aquarelle, but a more reasonable choice would be to take the escalator down to *Chen's,* a small walk-in restaurant in the Watergate's interior shopping mall, where you'll find out why Bob and Liddy go there for the lemon chicken. Chen's is located at 2542 Virginia Avenue NW. Call 965–4104. Inexpensive.

There are at least two good reasons to visit the ***Arts Club of Washington,*** an organization founded to promote the appreciation of art

Concerts, Compliments of the Kennedy

*A*lthough you'll want to join the many who tour the **Kennedy Center,** try to time your visit for 6:00 P.M. That's when, every day, there's a free concert given in the Center's Grand Foyer, and it could be almost anything from ballet to jazz. As Woody Allen once said about life itself, "all you have to do is turn up."

through a broad range of cultural programs and exhibits. The fifty-five parlors and public rooms of the club's headquarters exhibit paintings by local, national, and international artists and are the scene of a wide range of cultural programs that include literary readings and concerts. The house also contains period furnishings and an old-shoe, book-lined library that will take you back to 1916 when the club was founded. The club offers a free concert series at noon every Friday.

The club's headquarters, located in the Monroe House, one of the capital's oldest and most historic structures, is alone worth a visit. Built in 1806, this handsome Georgian mansion, later expanded to include the house next door, was the home of Secretary of State James Monroe in 1814; in 1817, when Monroe became president, this became the *de facto* White House until restoration of the Executive Mansion could be completed after the fire of 1814. The house was later the British Legation, until the club moved there in 1916.

The Arts Club, 2017 I Street NW (331–7282) is open Tuesday through Friday 10:00 A.M. to 5:00 P.M., Saturday 10:00 A.M. to 2:00 P.M.; closed Sundays. E-mail: artsclub@erols.com. Metro: Foggy Bottom or Farragut West (orange and blue lines).

PLACES TO STAY IN FOGGY BOTTOM

The George Washington University Inn, 824 New Hampshire Avenue NW; 337–6620 or (800) 426–4455, fax 298–7499, www.gwuinn.com. This well-furnished and well-run hotel is nicely positioned on a residential street close to both the Kennedy Center and the Foggy Bottom Metro stop. Its ninety-five rooms are split between suites and regular guest rooms. Moderate. Metro: Foggy Bottom (orange and blue lines).

Hotel Lombardy, 2019 Pennsylvania Avenue NW; 828–2600 or (800) 424–5486, www.hotellombardy.com. Unless you're looking for it, you might miss this European-style urban inn between downtown and Georgetown. Once an apartment house, the Lombardy has 127 well-appointed suites and guestrooms, many with kitchenettes and dining areas; the best rooms are on the renovated floors. As a bonus, it has the only attendant-operated, door cage elevator you're likely ever to find. Moderate. Metro: Foggy Bottom (orange and blue lines).

Wyndham Bristol Hotel, 2430 Pennsylvania Avenue NW; 955–6400, fax 955–5765. This European-style hotel predictably attracts many international visitors as well as performers who like its proximity to the Kennedy Center. Both Georgetown and downtown are a short walk away. Moderate. Metro: Foggy Bottom (orange and blue lines).

SUITE OR APARTMENT HOTELS

Conventional hotels attract the most visitor attention, but don't overlook the District's many suite hotels, especially if you're traveling with kids or like the idea of returning to the comfort of your own space after a long day of work or sightseeing. Some of the best are conveniently located in Foggy Bottom. All of the following offer well-appointed suites with kitchens. Prices are moderate, but ask about weekend and other special rates, of which there are many.

State Plaza Hotel, 2117 E Street NW; 861–8200 or (800) 424–2859. Convenient to the State Department, George Washington University, and the Kennedy Center. The hotel's moderately priced Garden Cafe, a definite find with an outdoor patio and top-notch American cuisine, is popular with American and foreign diplomats. Open Monday through Friday 7:00 A.M. to 3:00 P.M. and 5:00 to 10:00 P.M., Saturday and Sunday 8:00 to 11:00 A.M. and 5:00 to 10:00 P.M., Sunday brunch 10:00 A.M. to 2:00 P.M.

St. James, 950 24th Street NW; 457–0500 or (800) 852–8512, www.stjames suites.com. Handy to the Foggy Bottom Metro (orange and blue lines), the World Bank, and downtown. Great views and a swimming pool for those toasty Washington summers.

One Washington Circle Hotel, One Washington Circle NW; 872–1680 or (800) 424–9671, fax 887–4989, www.onewash-circlehotel.com. Overlooks Foggy Bottom Metro. The hotel's moderately priced restaurant, the West End Cafe, routinely draws praise from local food critics for its creative dishes. The cafe is open daily for breakfast, lunch, and dinner.

River Inn, 924 25th Street NW; 337–7600 or (800) 424–2741, fax: 337–6520, www.theriverinn.com, e-mail riverinn@erols.com. Don't be surprised if you find your fellow guests lugging tubas and cellos (this is where it pays to be a flutist); the River Inn is a favorite long-term hideaway for musicians, actors, and other performers at the Kennedy Center just up the street. Its cozy restaurant, the Foggy Bottom Cafe, is open Monday through Friday 7:00 to 10:00 A.M., 11:00 A.M. to 2:30 P.M., and 5:00 to 10:00 P.M., Saturday and Sunday 8:00 to 10:00 A.M., brunch 11:30 A.M. to 2:30 P.M., and 5:00 to 10:00 P.M.

PLACES TO EAT IN
FOGGY BOTTOM

Bristol Cafe, 2430 Pennsylvania Avenue NW; 955–6400. The excellent Bristol Cafe has great crab cakes and a lot of nice Italian-type things on the menu, along with a tranquil and elegant air. Open daily 6:30 A.M. to 11:00 P.M.; Sunday brunch is served from 11:00 A.M. to 2:30 P.M. Moderate. Metro: Foggy Bottom (orange and blue lines).

Donatello, 2514 L Street NW; 333–1485. The atmosphere in this two-story candlelit rendezvous is *Italiano romantico,* while the food, especially the great veal dishes and pastas, is *Italiano squisito.* Highly professional service, an outdoor patio for warm-weather dining, and a location on the border between Foggy Bottom and Georgetown make this a good all-round choice. Open for lunch Monday through Friday 11:30 A.M. to 2:30 P.M.; dinner Sunday through Thursday 5:00 to 11:30 P.M., until 12:30 A.M. on weekends. Moderate. Metro: Foggy Bottom (orange and blue lines).

Kinkead's, 2000 Pennsylvania Avenue NW; 296–7700. One of America's top food authorities recently wrote that, when in Washington, he could eat every meal at Kinkead's. That's no exaggeration—this American brasserie consistently makes the top of most everyone's list of places to dine in the capital. Everything is great, but Chef Robert Kinkead specializes in seafood dishes like Scandinavian salmon stew, baked halibut with crab and Virginia ham, or maybe something from the extensive raw bar. Sinful

---

Where to Find the Author's Favorite Places to Eat in Foggy Bottom

Chen's
2542 Virginia Avenue NW; 965–4104
(see page 79 for full listing)

---

desserts, Sunday brunch, and a world-class wine list too. Reservations essential. Expensive but worth it. Open daily 11:30 A.M. to 2:30 P.M. and 5:30 to 10:30 P.M. Metro: Foggy Bottom (orange and blue lines).

The Venetian Room and **Cafe Lombardy,** 2019 Pennsylvania Avenue NW; 828–2600. The intimate Venetian Room and the bright and informal Cafe Lombardy, both located in the Hotel Lombardy, are well worth visiting even if you're not a guest. Open daily 7:00 to 10:30 A.M., 11:30 A.M. to 2:30 P.M., and 5:30 to 9:30 P.M. Moderate. Metro: Foggy Bottom (orange and blue lines).

Zuki Moon, 824 New Hampshire Avenue NW; 337–6620. Located in the George Washington University Inn, this Japanese noodle restaurant has a topflight chef, and bowls full of acclaim and awards from local and national critics. Zuki Moon's meals in a bowl are just that, and the tempura and grilled fish are terrific. Open Monday through Friday 7:00 to 10:00 A.M., 11:00 A.M. to 2:30 P.M. and 5:00 to10:00 P.M., Saturday and Sunday 8:00 to 10:30 A.M. and 5:00 to 10:00 P.M. Moderate. Metro: Foggy Bottom (orange and blue lines).

Georgetown

A mix of smart shops, historic homes, and hip street life have made Georgetown one of Washington's liveliest and most desirable neighborhoods. But Georgetown was there first: Almost a century before the District of Columbia was created, Georgetown had a life of its own as a wealthy but inelegant Maryland river port that was the commercial gateway to the "west" (i.e., Ohio). In the eighteenth and early nineteenth centuries, an era that saw the founding of Georgetown University, Georgetown was also a slave-trading center and a key player in the tobacco trade at a time when tobacco was the lifeblood of the economy. The decline of the Chesapeake and Ohio Canal siphoned off the once-profitable Western trade and Georgetown fell on hard times, becoming, strange as its now seems, a smelly industrial town and one of Washington's worst slums. Georgetown was rescued in the 1930s when it was rediscovered and rehabilitated by officials of Roosevelt's New Deal. In the 1960s Georgetown was rediscovered all over again when President Kennedy's administration made it their headquarters and an enclave that became nationally known for a glittering lifestyle with chic dinner parties where Important People gathered to make Important Decisions.

Georgetown was a town in its own right until 1871, when it was incorporated into Washington, D.C., and its historic and evocative street names were lettered, numbered, and made part of the city's grid. Georgetown is not integrated into the city's Metro system, however, having opted out to avoid the congestion and crowds that residents thought the Metro would bring. Bad decision—both arrived anyway. Given the problems of parking on Georgetown's narrow streets, when you visit, either walk from the nearest Metro station, which is Foggy Bottom/ GWU (it'll take about twenty minutes), take a cab, or hop a Metrobus. Any of the 30-numbered buses (30, 32, 34, 35, 36) will take you from downtown to Georgetown; you can also transfer to these Metrobus routes from the Metro at 24th Street and Pennsylvania Avenue, near the Foggy Bottom stop. If you're coming from Dupont Circle, catch a D-2 or G-2 bus from 20th and P Streets.

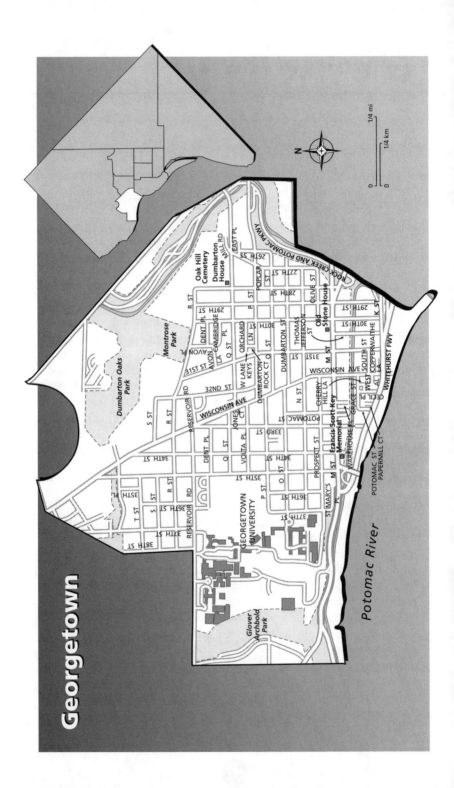

GEORGETOWN

TOP ATTRACTIONS IN GEORGETOWN

Dumbarton Oaks

Tudor Place

Dumbarton House

Riggs Riley House

The Old Stone House

Chesapeake and Ohio Canal

Smith Row

Although its main streets—M Street and Wisconsin Avenue—are definitely among Washington's well-worn tracks, this historic district offers a number of opportunities for visitors to leave the usual tourist treadmill behind and explore some often overlooked places that exude American culture and history.

One of them is **Dumbarton Oaks,** whose ultra-traditional Georgian facade conceals a surprising trove of pre-Columbian, Roman, and Byzantine treasures assembled by career diplomat Robert Woods Bliss and his wife, Mildred. In the mansion's pre-Columbian wing, dazzling Inca masks, necklaces, and plates of hammered gold from ancient Peruvian tombs compete for attention with radiant displays of Aztec artifacts of solid gold and jade. Incidentally, the museum building, designed by Philip Johnson, is itself a gem—an octagonal structure of glass, marble, teak, and bronze surrounding a lovely little garden and fountain.

Other rooms contain a priceless collection covering more than eleven centuries of Byzantine art: luminous bronzes, mosaics, and ivories that turn their display cases into jewel boxes. Its centerpiece is the magnificent Sion Treasure, a collection of liturgical silver from sixth-century Constantinople that lay hidden for fourteen centuries.

Most of Dumbarton Oaks is given over to staff offices and research libraries for Byzantine and pre-Columbian studies that are administered by Harvard, which was deeded the house, gardens, and collections in 1940. Visitors may, however, wander through the house's sumptuous music room, with El Greco's *Visitation,* tapestries, and memories of the 1944 Dumbarton Oaks Conferences, where the Allies planned and shaped the United Nations.

Lovers of fine gardens will also want to stroll through Dumbarton Oaks' ten acres of formal gardens, among America's best, and one of Washington's truly special places. The gardens unfold downhill on a series of broad terraces with colorful blooms that change with the seasons. Better yet, lots of tree-shaded walks and benches make the gardens an inviting R&R stop, but picnics are out. The Museum at Dumbarton Oaks, 1703 32nd Street NW (339–6400) is open Tuesday through Sunday 2:00 to 5:00 P.M.; suggested donation, $1.00. The garden entrance is at 31st and R Streets; open April through October 2:00 to 6:00 P.M.; November through May 2:00 to 5:00 P.M. Suggested donation, $4.00.

Back in 1816, when **Tudor Place** was completed, Georgetown was a thriving but noisy and disheveled tobacco port that Abigail Adams dismissed as "a dirty little hole." She could get pretty nasty, that Abigail, and she sure wouldn't say that today. While traffic and tumult may have lurked outside the massive gates of Tudor Place for nearly two centuries, this yellow stucco neoclassic mansion and its formal gardens have always been an oasis of urbanity and tranquillity.

Tudor Place was designed by William Thornton, the architect of the Octagon and the Capitol, for his friend Thomas Peter, a wealthy tobacco merchant and relative of Martha Washington. The Peter family then proceeded to make this estate their home for almost 200 years, which must be some kind of record for nomadic Americans. Through all of those years, Tudor Place was a distinguished home with distinguished visitors, including Robert E. Lee (also a Peter relative), Lafayette, and Henry Clay. Although it is one of Washington's finest Federal homes, Tudor Place is far from being a period house. The Peter family's long ownership and discerning tastes have created there a continuum of rarities acquired throughout the span of their occupancy, ranging from George Washington's furniture, silver, china, and other memorabilia to rare Oriental rugs and glass paintings collected in this century by Armistead Peter, the last of the family to reside there.

Before entering to start your guided tour, take a few minutes to see the mansion's historic North Garden, where, in azalea season, secluded walks lead to outbursts of showy whites and fiery pinks. But this southern formal garden, with its English boxwood hedges, also holds many year-round pleasures, including colorful magnolias, sprawling oaks

Foreign Intrigue at the Pig's Foot

*E*ven if you're not with the CIA, **Au Pied du Cochon,** at 1335 Wisconsin Avenue, is worth knowing about for its inexpensive French cooking, reasonably priced wines, and, in winter, a very nice cassoulet. But this Georgetown bistro became internationally famous in 1985, when KGB Colonel Vitaly Yurchenko redefected back to the Soviet Union during dinner, leaving his CIA escorts at the table on the pretext of going to the loo. The agents never knew until too late that Vitaly meant the one back at the Soviet Embassy. Well, Colonel Yurchenko is literally no longer with us, but Au Pied du Cochon lives on. A plaque marks the booth where this drama occurred (it's behind the second banquette from the left against the north wall). Open twenty-four hours. Inexpensive.

AUTHOR'S FAVORITES IN GEORGETOWN

Dumbarton Oaks

Chesapeake and Ohio Canal

Martin's Tavern

Clyde's

Wisconsin Avenue Shops

that saw the mansion's first days, and an elliptical bowling green that dates back to the early 1800s.

Once inside, you'll surely be taken by the elegant simplicity of the "Saloon," a sitting room with a two-story wall of concave windows and a staggering view out over the Potomac and Virginia. Outside, overlooking the south lawn, a columned rotunda creates a templelike porch that is Tudor Place's signature architectural feature.

Although the drawing rooms and parlors, with their priceless portraits and Colonial-era furniture, are splendid indeed, your real favorite is likely to be the mansion's handsome dining room, where chairs that once belonged to George Washington grace a grand mahogany table set with gleaming silver and period china. Upstairs all visitors, especially those from the other side of the Potomac, are thrilled to see the guest room and four-poster that Robert E. Lee used on his frequent visits. Tudor Place is located at 1644 31st Street NW; 965–0400. The Tudor Place Web site, www.tudorplace.org, carries a schedule of special events, including lectures and art exhibits. House tours are Tuesday through Friday at 10:00 and 11:30 A.M. and at 2:30 P.M. Saturday tours are given every hour from 10:00 A.M. to 4:00 P.M. The garden is open Monday through Saturday 10:00 A.M. to 4:00 P.M. Suggested donations: $6.00 for the house, $2.00 for the garden.

Architectural historians view **Dumbarton House** (not to be confused with Dumbarton Oaks) as a perfect example of the great Georgian manor houses built by wealthy Washington and tidewater Virginia merchants during the late 1700s. However, you'll probably remember it more for its wonderful collection of American cabinetry and furniture-making. In the library there's a gleaming secretary bookcase from 1775 New York, flanked by a pair of English globes showing the world of 1800. And if you want to see what Georgetown's busy port looked like in 1789, take a look at the background of the Peale portrait of the Stoddert children in the dining room.

In the music room, where women guests were exiled after dinner while husbands talked serious stuff, a 1795 Pembroke table is set for tea, consolation, perhaps, for missing all that early American guy talk; across the room a harp, piano, and violin of the same era stand ready for an eighteenth-century musicale.

In the upstairs bedroom you'll see that Washington political kitsch didn't begin with those Jack and Jackie drugstore plates when you spot the allegorical print of *America Paying Homage to France,* showing a native American princess in full headdress saluting an elegantly reclining France. This print was, *naturellement,* made in Paris. In addition to its elegant furnishings, Dumbarton House is the headquarters of the National Society of Colonial Dames. Dumbarton House, 2715 Q Street NW (337–2288), conducts forty-five-minute tours Tuesday through Saturday at 10:15 and 11:15 A.M. and 12:15 P.M. Closed between Christmas and New Year's and August through Labor Day. Suggested donation is $3.00.

Next to Dumbarton House, tucked away on the grassy space behind the apartment house at 27th and Q Streets, is *Mt. Zion Cemetery,* the oldest predominantly black burial ground in Washington. The property originated in 1809 as a cemetery for slaves and freedmen, as opposed to the ritzy whites-only Oak Hill Cemetery visible next door. Mt. Zion was neglected for years, and its wooden markers disappeared; trustees, however, have removed most of the remaining grave markers, which have been recorded and stored pending eventual restoration of this historic site as a memorial to the historic and large black presence in Georgetown. If you look carefully at the back of the cemetery, you'll find the redbrick underground vault used as a hideout for slaves escaping north to freedom on the Underground Railroad.

The *Mt. Zion United Methodist Church,* at 1334 29th Street NW, is the oldest African-American congregation in the District, having been organized in 1816 by slaves and freedmen of Georgetown's thriving black community that were subjected to segregation by their original, mainly white church. The first Mt. Zion Church, which was a major stop on the Underground Railroad, burned down in 1880. Over the

The "Social Safeway"

*T*he seemingly standard mega-grocery at 1855 Wisconsin gets its nickname from the Washington notables who flock there. Where else are you going to routinely find cabinet officers squeezing the lemons, pundits prowling the produce, or a certain very well-known TV news anchor sniffing the cantaloupe? The Safeway is also a meeting place for zillions of single Georgetowners who over the years have met, not really by chance, among the cleansers or condiments, then made plans for dinner, a movie, and who knows what else. I once spotted Elizabeth Taylor shopping at the Social Safeway and still haven't gotten over it. Visiting hours: 6:00 A.M. to 11:00 P.M. daily. Black tie optional.

Art and Antiques on M Street

Yo'll find some of Washington's top galleries and antiques stores along M Street, in the blocks between 28th and 30th Streets. Among the best:

- **Grafix,** 2904 M, for vintage posters and an encyclopedic collection of New Yorker and Fortune covers dating back to the '20s. Ask to see the posters for the long-vanished transatlantic luxury liners of the '30s and '40s. Open Monday through Friday 11:00 A.M. to 6:00 P.M., Saturday 11:00 A.M. to 5:00 P.M. Call 342–0610.

- **Janis Aldridge,** at 2900 M, specializes in rare botanical and architectural prints, along with antique European silver and furniture. Open Tuesday through Saturday 10:00 A.M. to 6:00 P.M. Call 338–7710.

- **Spectrum Gallery,** around the corner at 1132 29th Street, sells colorful posters and prints, along with a selection of nice oils and photographs. Open Tuesday through Saturday noon to 6:00 P.M., Sunday noon to 5:00 P.M. Call 333–0954.

- **J. K. S. Bush,** at 2826 M, is a wonderland of formal antique furniture (mainly British and American), grandfather clocks, and paintings from the eighteenth and early nineteenth century. Open 10:00 A.M. to 6:00 P.M. Call 965–0653.

- **Bridge Street Books,** 2814 Pennsylvania Avenue, is one of those bookstores every neighborhood should be so lucky to have. This one's for lovers of serious nonfiction, heavy on politics, literature, history, and film; remainders table out front. Open Monday through Friday 11:00 A.M. to 10:00 P.M., Saturday until 11:00 P.M., Sunday noon to 7:00 P.M. Call 965–5200.

years many of the black parishioners either had moved away or were, before that, "sold to Georgia traders," but Mt. Zion retains its unique character. Its historic role in Georgetown's African-American community is commemorated in its **Heritage Center,** a cozy English cottage built in 1810 and located just around the corner at 2906 O Street. Admission to the Heritage Center and its archives is by appointment only; to set up a visit call 337–6711.

As you wander around on the east side of Wisconsin Avenue, you'll find plenty of mansions and row houses you'd like to wrap up and take home, but keep an eye out for some really special places such as the **Colonial House,** at 1305 30th Street, home of Miss Lydia English's tony finishing school for wealthy young women until the Civil war, when the army threw out the girls and brought the wounded of Bull Run there to recuperate. The building was later turned into an apartment house, which it is today.

Pleased as Punch

A plaque on the wall at 1054 31st Street commemorates Herman Hollerith, hardly a household name, but this gifted inventor launched the computer age from his workshop on this site. In 1880 Hollerith invented the punch card tabulating machine, after getting the idea of storing data on punched cards by watching a train conductor punch tickets. His machines took off in a big way, especially when the government used them to replace hundreds of clerks and save months of labor in tabulating the 1890 census. Still wondering why you should be interested in all this? To help you sort it out, I'll just mention that, in the early 1920s, Hollerith's Computer Tabulating Machine Company changed its name to International Business Machines.

In the backyard of *2726 N Street,* you'll find a large and beautiful Chagall mosaic on the back wall of the garden. The story is that Marc Chagall was a close friend of the owner and, after a visit, bestowed this wonderful gift on his host. You and I should be so lucky. The mosaic is best viewed from the 28th Street sidewalk. The house also has a handsome bronze sculpture in its front garden.

The *Riggs Riley House* at 3038 N Street is a splendid Federal home built in 1816 by a prominent banker, but better known more recently as the home of Averell Harriman and his wife, Pamela. The Harrimans turned the house over to their friend Jackie Kennedy after President Kennedy's assassination. After living there a month, she bought the house across the street at 3017 N Street.

If it weren't for the limited hours, you could spend an entire day in *Booked Up,* the antiquarian bookshop that looks like the Georgetown equivalent of an eighteenth-century London study. The shop's handsome walnut bookshelves contain a collection of modern first editions and a wide range of travel books and guides, including the greatest of them all, the vintage Baedekers that everyone used during the golden age of travel between 1870 and 1930. And if you're especially lucky, Booked Up's owner, best-selling author Larry McMurtry, will help you find what you're looking for. Booked Up, upstairs at 1204 31st Street, is open 11:00 A.M. to 3:00 P.M. on weekdays, 10:30 A.M. to 2:00 P.M. on Saturday. Call 965–3244; fax 298–6555.

The *Old Stone House,* at 3051 M Street, is Washington's oldest dwelling. The house started out in 1765 as a cabinetmaker's workshop, after which it was used variously as either a private home or place of business. It's now run by the National Park Service, which uses it as a small house museum of pre-Revolutionary life, with the spinning wheels and furniture of the period; check to see about taking in one of the frequent craft demonstrations. The House's garden/orchard makes a great place to take it easy or even picnic with the locals. Open Wednesday through Sunday 10:00 A.M. to 4:00 P.M.; 426–6851.

Washington's legendary **Blues Alley,** true to its name, is tucked away off the alley at 1073 Wisconsin Avenue. World-class jazz artists like Wynton Marsalis, Benny Green, and Nancy Wilson have performed there, which is one reason that the *New York Times* called it "the nation's finest supper club." The food is almost as good as the music, which is saying a lot. With all this good stuff going on, you must reserve by calling 337–4141. Open seven days a week, with nightly shows from 8:00 to 10:00 and a third show at midnight on Friday and Saturday. Dinner from 6:00 P.M.

With a little historical imagination, you can get a sense of the long-vanished port of Georgetown at the corner of Wisconsin Avenue and K Street, which 200 years ago was the heart of the town's busy waterfront. This cluster of redbrick commercial buildings is the Old Dodge Warehouse, which was built in 1800 next to the Potomac docks as warehouses for Havana "seegars," Cuban molasses, Santo Domingo coffee, and the other cargoes of a busy port.

Washington Harbour, on the Georgetown waterfront at 3000 K Street, between 29th and 31st, is a major residential and office complex that will interest you chiefly for its lively restaurant scene and riverside promenade. In good weather it's great fun to dine outside next to the Potomac and gaze out at the Lincoln Memorial and the Kennedy Center. Across the way is Theodore Roosevelt Island, now a wooded park but once an important Civil War encampment used for the defense of Washington. But it's the river that's the big attraction for diners, who enjoy the nonstop aquatic pageant of racing sculls from Georgetown and other schools, frequent sightseeing ships, and possibly a luxury yacht or cabin cruiser.

You have several Washington Harbor restaurants to choose from. **Sequoia** (944–4200) with a large glassed-in dining room and lots of action at the outside bar and tables, is open Monday through Saturday 11:30 A.M. to 3:30 P.M., Sunday 5:30 to 11:30 P.M. With a weekend brunch from 10:00 A.M. to 3:30 P.M. Moderate. **Tony and Joe's** (944–4545) serves seafood specialties (none from the Potomac) daily from 11:00 A.M. to 10:00 P.M. Expensive. The Italian-leaning **Riverside Grille** (342–3535) is open Monday through Friday 11:30 A.M. to 11:00 P.M., until midnight Friday and Saturday. Moderate.

In season, which is April to November, you won't want to miss the *Canal Clipper,* a replica of an early canal boat, for a ride on the **Chesapeake and Ohio Canal,** which is now a National Historic Park. During these hour-long mule-drawn excursions, you'll pass through locks and hear from period-costumed guides. You'll also see some of the Canal's original warehouses, built in 1828 and now reincarnated as sales and office space, and you'll envy the Washingtonians who jog, bicycle, or amble along the towpath. The *Clipper* hurtles along at speeds reaching 4 miles per hour, so fasten those seat belts! Although you'll enjoy the leisurely pace, the slow speed is the reason that the canal, which was conceived as a 185-mile freight artery connecting the port of Georgetown with the West, never panned out commercially, losing out to the railroads despite the political and financial support of heavy hitters like George Washington and Thomas Jefferson. No reservations, but to hear more, call the Park Service at 653–5190 for sailing times, which vary during the season. Get your tickets at the Visitor Center at the rear of 1057 Thomas Jefferson Street: $7.50 for adults, $4.00 for children. The Visitor Center is open in season from 9:00 A.M. to 4:30 P.M. and from November to March on weekends only 10:00 A.M. to 4:00 P.M.

On your walk up **Wisconsin Avenue,** you'll find a profusion of stores with the usual names offering the usual running shoes, designer jeans, and legible clothing. But if you look selectively you'll be rewarded with

The Tomb of the Well-Known Mascot

*T*his is very weird, but you shouldn't leave Washington without knowing about that stone tablet on the wall of 1066 Wisconsin that memorializes a dog. This was not just your everyday pooch, but "Bush, the Old Fire Dog," beloved mascot of the Vigilant Volunteer Fire Company, which occupied this site in the 1860s. Bush died in July 1869 under mysterious circumstances, probably poisoned by a rival fire company in a day of cutthroat competition between the city's firefighters. Although RIP is inscribed on the tablet, the site of Bush's grave is not definitely known; a recent Washington Flyer story speculates that the murdered mutt was buried by his bereaved owners under the firehouse, minus his tail, which for years was reverently kept in the firehouse in a glass case. The building is the oldest firehouse in the city; over the door you can still see the "V" for Vigilant. Today it is home to Papa Razzi, a popular Italian restaurant. If you ask about Bush's tail, they will smirk, then deny knowing anything about it. Obviously, this is another Washington cover-up.

Paddle Your Own Canoe

If gazing at the Potomac and the C&O Canal has started you thinking about your own nautical expedition, you're in luck. At **Jack's Boathouse,** at 3500 K Street, not far from the foot of Wisconsin Avenue, you can rent a canoe or kayak and paddle the Potomac for $10 an hour or $30 per day. Just be sure to get some river safety instructions first—the Potomac can be hazardous. Jack's is open between April 1 and November 1 from 8:00 A.M. to sunset. Call 337–9642. Those massive stone pilings just beyond Jack's parking lot are the foundations of the Aqueduct Bridge, which once carried Canal barges across the Potomac to Virginia. In Civil War times it became the main land bridge to the Confederacy.

Fletcher's Boat House is farther away; you can either drive or, better yet, walk there from Georgetown along the C&O Canal towpath, which will take about forty minutes. When you arrive you'll find one-stop shopping for recreation involving the Potomac or the Canal. Fletcher's will rent you a canoe ($8.00 an hour, $18.00 per day), kayak ($8.50 an hour, $21.00 per day), or rowboat ($8.00 and $16.00). Fletcher's also rents bikes to ride the towpath for $8.00 an hour (two-hour minimum) or $12.00 per day. If it's shad or stripers you're after, Fletcher's sells D.C. fishing licenses, tackle, and bait. There's also a small snack bar and large picnicking area. Fletcher's, at 4940 Canal Road at Reservoir Road NW (244–0461), is open daily 7:30 A.M. to dusk from mid-March to Thanksgiving.

visits to the fine specialty shops and restaurants for which Georgetown has long been renowned.

Start just below the intersection of Wisconsin and M at **Ching Ching Cha,** a corner of perfect repose and serenity on busy Wisconsin Avenue Ching Ching Cha, a Chinese teahouse, has everything for the lover of fine teas and the ancient rituals that go with them. The shop serves and sells every kind of tea imaginable, along with tea meals of miso salmon and curried chicken and a wide assortment of kettles, cups, and other tea paraphernalia you'll need to hold a special tea ceremony in your own home. If that's your plan, you'd better snaffle up a few of Ching Ching Cha's low rosewood tables and pillows, then figure out how to slip them into your car or onto the plane. Tea with sweets and dumplings are served on those tables Monday through Friday 2:30 to 5:30 P.M. Ching Ching Cha, at 1063 Wisconsin Avenue NW (333–8288), is open daily 11:30 A.M. to 10:00 P.M.

Martin's Tavern has been a Georgetown tradition since it opened in 1933, which in Washington restaurant years is equal to being in town since the Van Buren administration. In the '50s, when they lived just up

Stars and Fire Marks

*O*n the walls of many old Georgetown buildings you'll spot large metal stars, which were not meant just to be decorative. Instead these "rod stars" secured the ends of iron poles that ran through each end of a building and held them together.

As you stroll through Georgetown you'll also see little oval plaques on the walls of many houses, some with a hose, tree, or eagle, each symbol representing a different insurance company. Those "fire marks" indicated to volunteer firemen that the house was insured, thus assuring them that they'd be rewarded for saving that home. History records a number of occasions when firemen allowed uninsured houses to burn or even, some say, would themselves do a little selective torching.

N Street, Martin's was Jack and Jackie's neighborhood hangout. The Kennedys, like today's regulars, probably liked Martin's clubhouse atmosphere where Tiffany glass drop lamps hang over cozy wooden booths and where patrons order real drinks like Martinis or Scotch. Martin's menu is also special—where else these days can you find comfort food like the elusive Welsh rarebit or shepherd's pie and local specialties like shad roe and first-rate crab cakes? And the hamburgers just might be the best in the city. Also great for breakfast and weekend brunch. Martin's Tavern, at Wisconsin Avenue and N Street NW (333–7370), is open Monday through Thursday 10:00 A.M. to 11:00 P.M., Friday 10:00 A.M. to midnight, Saturday 8:30 A.M. to midnight, Sunday 8:30 A.M. to 11:00 P.M. Moderate.

Random Harvest is the place to find antique furniture, including American-made hutches and tables of pine, along with a wide selection of vintage prints, especially botanicals. The store also offers distinctive outdoor chairs, tables, and cachepots and a lot of other excuses to start furnishing your garden. You'll also find fancier furniture here, such as commodes with wood inlaid tops and maybe even a huge bed with posts that look like those pillars in St. Peter's in the Vatican. Random Harvest, at 1313 Wisconsin (333–5569), is open Monday through Wednesday 11:00 A.M. to 6:00 P.M., Thursday and Friday 11:00 A.M. to 8:00 P.M., Saturday 11:00 A.M. to 6:00 P.M., and Sunday from noon to 6:00 P.M.

The *Old Forest Bookshop,* just off Wisconsin at 3145 Dumbarton Street (965–3842), is a great place to browse for used, out-of-print and hard-to-find books, and the store is full of them. The accent here is on serious stuff, mainly history, literature, and art, with a lot of books of the "coffee table" variety. If you have some scarce books you want to sell (not this one, please) they'll also be happy to talk to you. Open Monday through Saturday 11:00 A.M. to 6:30 P.M., Sunday noon to 6:00 P.M.

If you shop at *Baldaquin,* you'll not only sleep better, but you might (no offense meant) even smell better. This shop specializes in the finest imported linens, duvet covers, and sheets from top European foreign producers such as Pratesi, Frette, and Porthault, and carries a definitely upscale line of French bath oils and gels. Proprietor Lisa Mullins Thompson will also sell you the bed of your dreams, perhaps one hand-made and carved by Simon Horn, said to be England's top bedmaster (if that's a real word). If all this nighttime luxury is making you think harder about marriage, Ms. Thompson will happily help you assemble your gift registry because "Baldaquin is changing the way Washingtonians are getting married," a goal not to be snoozed at. Baldaquin, 1413 Wisconsin Avenue NW (625–1600, www.baldaquin.com), is open Monday through Saturday 10:00 A.M. to 6:00 P.M.

Although Baldaquin features the work of European craftsmen, at *Appalachian Spring* the emphasis is strictly all-American, with works by homegrown designers and craftspeople. This is the place to find a huge assortment of cutting boards and other housewares of hand-carved woods, along with handmade designer pottery and ceramics. Appalachian Spring's artisan collection also features textiles, including

Tours for Voyeurs

*I*f you're frustrated at not being able to peek inside all those splendid Georgetown homes, try to arrange your visit for the weekend after Easter and take the annual **Georgetown House Tour,** the only time that some of the neighborhood's finest homes open their doors to visitors. The tour takes visitors to six homes on Satur-day; six more are open the following day. Tickets are $25 per person per day, but $45 buys you both days of gawking and envy; a sumptuous after-noon tea at St. John's Church is included in the ticket price. Children under ten are not permitted. To order tickets, call 338–1796, ext. 50 or fax 338–3921. Tickets may also be ordered on the Internet at www.georgetown housetour.com.

If you're interested in flowers, the first Saturday in May is **Georgetown Gar-den Day,** when self-guided tours will take you to twelve of Georgetown's finest private gardens. Garden Day hours are 10:30 A.M. to 5:00 P.M. Tick-ets cost $20 and can be purchased by turning up at Christ Church, 31st and O Streets, on the day of the tour, or reserved by e-mailing gtwngarden day@aol.com.

colorful place mats, quilts, and rag dolls for the kids. Appalachian Spring, 1415 Wisconsin Avenue (337–5780), is open Monday through Friday 10:00 A.M. to 8:00 P.M., Saturday 10:00 A.M. to 6:00 P.M., and Sunday noon to 6:00 P.M.

Waterworks, a.k.a. bathroom central, at 1519 Wisconsin, is proof that your bathroom doesn't have to be a water closet. This store will sell you the classy bathroom gear you've always coveted, like those great European bathtub faucets with showerheads that look like vintage telephone handsets, and great porcelain claw-footed tubs. Accessories include chrome soap dishes and shaving mirrors. Waterworks' ceramics collection features colorful porcelain washbowls and a broad selection of very snazzy bathroom wall tiles (sorry, no thrones). Waterworks (333–7180, www.waterworks.net) is open Monday through Friday 9:00 A.M. to 5:00 P.M., Saturday until 4:00 P.M.; closed Sunday.

If there's any store that rates the title "Georgetown institution," it's **Little Caledonia,** a treasure trove that is wall to wall, floor to ceiling with lovely things. Here you'll wander through a maze of elegant ceramics and china settings, antique furniture and mirrors, ceramic animals, prints, and a lot of other things you might not have thought about. The back room is full of fine fabrics and even wallpaper. In December the shop offers a fine selection of Victorian glass Christmas ornaments. Little Caledonia, 1419 Wisconsin Avenue NW (333–4700), is open Monday through Saturday 10:00 A.M. to 6:00 P.M., Sunday noon to 5:00 P.M.

A few steps from Wisconsin Avenue, at 3235 P Street, the **Georgetown Gallery of Art** presents a mix of new talents with established greats like Picasso and Chagall. It's almost certain that you'll also find works by British sculptor and artist Henry Moore (a friend of the gallery's late founder, Lee Silberstein), who sells his works directly to the gallery. Open Tuesday through Saturday 11:00 A.M. to 5:00 P.M. Call 333–6308.

Flea Market, Georgetown Style

*A*ddicted to flea markets? Georgetown's may not be the cheapest you've ever seen, but it's probably one of the toniest and most socially acceptable. This is just the place to pick up Muffy and Jason's castoffs, along with a lot of other stuff. You'll find it across from the "Social Safeway," natch, in the schoolyard at the corner of Wisconsin and 34th. Open Sunday 9:00 A.M. to 5:00 P.M.

The Gun Barrel Fence

Just beyond the gallery, at 3241 P Street, you'll find another excellent bookseller, the **Bryn Mawr Lantern Bookshop,** which lives up to its name by operating for the benefit of the famous college. This bright and attractive shop is well stocked with lightly used books and well run by volunteer staff, all of whom would be happy to see you walk in with a few hundred books to donate to their favorite cause. Open Monday through Friday 11:00 A.M. to 4:00 P.M., Saturday 11:00 A.M. to 5:00 P.M., Sunday noon to 5:00 P.M. Call 333–3222.

Good fences make good neighbors, and gun barrel fences make the best neighbors of all. That's probably what gunsmith Reuben Daw thought when, in 1850, he snapped up some Mexican War surplus gun barrels, spiked the muzzles, and made a fence for his house at 2811 P Street.

Back on Wisconsin Avenue, *Patisserie Poupon,* at number 1645, is a great place to know about for a break or a light lunch. Favorites include light salads, a plate of charcuterie, or a chocolate cake that will provide a sugar surge powerful enough to last until at least the next shop, *A Mano,* at 1677 Wisconsin, where, for a few bucks (well, maybe more than a few) you can buy yourself the snazziest ceramics in town. True to its name, A Mano specializes in handmade tableware, especially Italian majolica and French faience; it also carries a broad selection of linens and decorative objects, including wonderful cachepots and rooster-head wine carafes from Umbrian workshops. Open Monday through Saturday 10:00 A.M. to 6 P.M., Sunday noon to 5:00 P.M. Call 298–7200.

Because it's small and surrounded by private homes, you might over-look *J. F. Ptak Science Books,* at the corner of Volta Place and 33rd Street. That would be too bad, because you'd have missed one of the country's best and largest collections of antiquarian books on the phys-ical sciences and certainly one of Washington's most interesting and eclectic stores. Mr. Ptak's book inventory, which exceeds 100,000 titles, is especially strong on the history of computers and science astro-physics, science biography, and mathematical theory. This is also just the place to ask about picking up those wax medical models you've always wanted, along with early twentieth-century impressionist pho-tographs or naval engineering drawings from the Civil War. The store also reflects Ptak's interest in graphical display of information, with its large collection of antiquarian maps, photographs, and prints. J. F. Ptak Science Books, 1531 33rd Street NW (337–0945, www.thesciencebook store.com), is open Tuesday through Saturday noon to 5:00 P.M.

For a perfect example of Georgetown's ability to come up with hidden nooks and crannies, stick your head into *Pomander Walk,* a tiny dead-end mews just off Volta Place between 33rd and 34th Streets. Pomander Walk, which consists of ten cozy row houses, each painted a different

Camelot on the Potomac

*J*ack Kennedy loved Georgetown and lived there in five different houses. As a freshman Congressman, the future President established bachelor quarters at 1528 31st Street, then, after his 1950 election to the Senate, moved to 1400 34th Street. As newlyweds, Jack and Jackie set up their first Georgetown home at 3271 P Street. Later in his Senatorial term the Kennedys rented the house at 2808 P Street. Jack and Jackie's longest residence in Georgetown was at 3307 N Street, where they lived from 1957 until they moved to 1600 Pennsylvania Avenue. The doorstop of the N Street house became famous as the place where the President-elect announced his cabinet choices. Across the street, on the wall at 3302 N Street, you'll see the plaque presented to the owner by a White House press corps grateful for the shelter, coffee, and doughnuts she supplied them during their long waits for Kennedy's appearances during the icy winter of 1960–61.

pastel color, started out as Bell's Court, a group of homes rented by African-American laborers and named for inventor Alexander Graham Bell, who lived in the neighborhood and owned a sizable chunk of nineteenth-century Georgetown. It's hard to believe now, but these charming dwellings were condemned in the 1950s; thanks to Georgetown's post–World War II housing boom, they were rescued and restored.

At 34th Street think about turning left and heading downhill to O Street, a leafy (and bumpy—the residents like it that way) cobblestone street where you'll see the peculiar tracks of Georgetown's long-vanished cable-powered streetcar system. O Street is also lined with fine homes, each of which, in a place as old as Georgetown, has a past.

The gaudiest history, however, may belong to the ***Bodisco House*** at 3322 O, named for Baron Alexander de Bodisco, Russian ambassador to the United States from 1837 until 1854. Bodisco was probably a terrific diplomat and surely a credit to the czar, but is remembered today for his remarkable marriage to Washingtonian Harriet Williams. The wedding took place in this house in June 1839, when Bodisco was sixty-three ("short and stout with . . . a shining brown wig") and Harriet was lovely and sixteen. More than a few eyebrows were raised, but that didn't keep the ceremony from being a high point of the Georgetown social season, with Washington glitterati like President Van Buren, Henry Clay, and the entire diplomatic corps in attendance, proving once again that official and social Washington will turn out for almost anything. Defying all bets and leers, this April-December couple, delicately referred to at the time as "Beauty and the Beast," apparently got along very well, producing six children. The Bodisco house became a Washington social center famous for its lavish and frequent entertaining. When the Baron died in 1854, he was buried in Georgetown's Oak Hill cemetery under an obelisk proclaiming his full titles. As for Harriet, she married the British military attaché, presumably another beauty, and lived happily ever after (again). Unfortunately, the Bodisco House is not open to the public.

Thomas Jefferson contributed $50 to the cost of building *St. John's Episcopal Church,* at 3240 O Street, a quintessential Colonial church in the Federal style. Dolley Madison was a regular at St. John's, as was Francis Scott Key. The church building was started in 1796 and opened in 1804. Since then, the church and its adjoining parish house have undergone a few modifications, but retain their clean, classic lines and the original "pepper pot" belfry. Inside this classic, spare high-ceilinged church are fine stained glass windows and, unexpectedly, a mosaic floor that will remind you more of Rome than of Washington. The door to the church's rustic Chapel of the Carpenter is around the corner on Potomac Street. Ring for admission.

From Potomac Street, walk down to N Street and some superb Federal-style homes, which have remained practically unchanged since the time they were built between 1815 and 1818. As you walk past *Smith Row,* from number 3255 to 3267, and *Cox's Row,* from 3327 to 3339 in the next block, take a look at the wonderful details in these elegant homes—the handsome doorways and fanlights, the dormers, and the recessed swags on each facade. John Cox, the Mayor of Georgetown who built Cox's Row, turned 3337 over to the Marquis de Lafayette during the 1824 visit when Lafayette Square was named for him. Between the two rows, at 3307 N, stands the Marbury House, where John F. Kennedy lived when he was elected president.

The Capital's first public market was built at 3276 M Street in 1795, then replaced in 1865 by the current historic landmark. The building's original fish mongers, butchers, and produce sellers have long since taken their wares to the Big Market in the Sky, but their much more genteel successors, *Dean and Deluca,* carry on in a market sure to remind you of those great European food halls and their enticing pyramids of lovely fruit and carefully arranged fish and meat. Just don't expect those 1795 prices or the veal deal that Thomas Jefferson got when he shopped here in 1806. Although he may have been a tired shopper, Jefferson didn't get to order a gourmet sandwich at the indoor/outdoor cafe, but you can.

PLACES TO STAY IN GEORGETOWN

The Latham Hotel, 3000 M Street NW; 726–5000. This small European-style hotel is located right on Georgetown's main drag, but only a few steps from the tranquillity of the C&O Canal. No mistake about it, this is a first-class hotel with first-class service and amenities, and you'll pay accordingly. Not only that, the Latham's in-house restaurant, Citronelle, is among the best in the capital, if not the nation. Much less pricey is the attached La Madeleine restaurant, which is a French-style cafeteria (when was the last time you visited one of those?) and a good one. The Latham is expensive.

The Georgetown Inn, 1310 Wisconsin Avenue NW; 333–8900. This Olde Georgetowne inn is Colonial only when it comes to the decor in its rooms—four-poster beds, faux Sheraton furniture, and brass lamps—but the amenities and services are pure twenty-first century. Downstairs there's an outpost of the California-based Daily Grille, which means great salads and steaks. The inn is expensive; the Daily Grill isn't.

Georgetown Suites, 1111 30th Street NW; 298–7800. As its name tells you, this is an all-suite hotel located just off M Street, next to bus lines that will take you everywhere you want to go, including the nearest Metro stop. Also handy to the Canal and Washington Harbour. Suites come with full kitchens, but if you don't feel like making breakfast, go down to the lobby for the complimentary continental breakfast bar. Moderate.

Hotel Monticello, 1075 Thomas Jefferson Street NW; 337–0900. Georgetown's newest hotel, opened in early 2000, the Monticello is an intimate boutique inn with forty-seven wonderfully furnished suites and a central location in Georgetown. It won't be cheap, but if you're looking for the convenience of upscale suite hotel living with more than a whiff of a small European hotel, this is a real possibility. Expensive.

PLACES TO EAT IN GEORGETOWN

Sen5es, 3206 Grace Street NW; 342–9083. No, that's not a typo, the 5 in the middle represents the five senses, each of which will be very happily engaged in this luminous, serene bakery/restaurant. Try a terrific risotto, pan-roasted sea bass, or maybe a roasted venison chop; then sample the Black Forest cake or another irresistible dessert. Open Tuesday through Sunday 8:00 A.M. to 2:30 P.M., and 6:00 to 10:00 P.M. Afternoon tea and pastries are served Tuesday through Sunday 3:00 to 5:00 P.M. Closed Monday. Moderate.

La Ruche, 1039 31st Street NW; 965–2684, www.cafe-laruche.com. There's a nice Gallic feel about this out-of-the-way and unpretentious "beehive" near the Potomac's left bank. You can choose between hefty salads, rich onion and other soups, and light fare, including *croque monsieur* and grilled chicken. The desserts are ethereal. Open Monday through Friday 11:30 A.M. to 10:30 P.M., Saturday and Sunday 10:00 A.M. to 11:30 P.M. Brunch is served Saturday and Sunday from 10:00 A.M. to 3:00 P.M. Inexpensive.

La Chaumiere, 2813 M Street NW; 338–1784. This combination of provincial French bistro and Georgetown institution has a corps of high-powered regular diners that could staff an entire administration. The price you'd pay, however, would be traces of *choucroute garni* on the treaties, onion soup stains on the legislation, and the remains of a memorable crab-filled crepe on the inaugural speech. Considering the usual quality of Washington's legislation and the exacting standards of La Chaumiere's kitchen, this would be an excellent trade-off indeed. Moderate. Reservations suggested. Open Monday through Friday 11:30 A.M. to 2:30 P.M. and Monday through Saturday 5:30 to 10:30 P.M. Moderate.

Tahoga, 2815 M Street NW; 338–5380. Tahoga may be the American Indian name for the settlement that is now Georgetown, but believe me, you're not going to find any Anacostian specialties at this winner of multiple local and national awards. Lovers of roast possum and pemmican will just have to dine elsewhere. This Tahoga offers a combination of New American and American Eclectic, with dishes like duck lasagna, braised lamb shank, meat loaf, and bourbon-glazed pork chops. The bright and airy rooms are a bonus, as is the little outside courtyard, which even Old Guys find romantic. With all that great food, soothing decor, and atmosphere, you knew it would be expensive. Open Monday through Friday 11:00 A.M. to 2:00 P.M. and 5:30 to 10:00 P.M., weekends 5:30 to 11:00 P.M. Reservations are essential. Expensive.

Bistro Lepic, 1736 Wisconsin Avenue; 333–0111. It's easy to imagine you're dining on the Left Bank at this small, bright restaurant lined with lively oils and prints. It's a big favorite with locals seeking super French cooking at a reasonable price. My favorite is the loin of lamb with truffles, but you might prefer the salmon in potato crust or the beef medallions with polenta. Good wine list too. Reservations are essential. Open daily 11:30 A.M. to 2:30 P.M., Monday through Thursday 5:30 to 10:00 P.M., until 10:30 on Friday and Saturday, 9:30 on Sunday. Moderate.

Clyde's, 3236 M Street NW; 333–9180. If there's one Georgetown restaurant that almost everybody likes it's Clyde's. This landmark restaurant gets the Oscar for longevity by staying in business since 1963, when JFK was president and nightlife on M Street consisted of a few bars like the Silver Dollar Cafe. (On amateur night, at the Silver Dollar, an elderly and none too sober gent in a greasy Uncle Sam suit frequently tapdanced on stilts.) Clyde's is still an outstanding neighborhood saloon that also attracts a national clientele of visitors. The reason is the convivial bar and a consistently first-rate kitchen that turns out great American stuff from burgers to crab cakes and inventive salads and fish dishes, plus a notable Sunday brunch. It's a lively scene, so reserve. Open Monday through Friday 11:30 A.M. to 2:00 A.M., weekends 10:00 A.M. to 2:00 A.M. Moderate.

Where to Find the Author's Favorite Places to Eat in Georgetown

Sequoia
Located at Washington Harbour; 944–4200
(see page 91 for full listing)

Tony and Joe's
Located at Washington Harbour; 944–4545
(see page 91 for full listing)

Riverside Grille
Located at Washington Harbour; 342–3535
(see page 91 for full listing)

Patisserie Poupon
1645 Wisconsin Avenue; 298–7200
(see page 97 for full listing)

Upper Northwest

The Upper Northwest covers a lot of territory, extending in a broad outer arc that starts along the Potomac just north of Georgetown and swings around above Dupont Circle, Adams Morgan, and Shaw, and ends at North Capitol Street, which divides Northwest from Northeast. Along the way it encompasses many of residential Washington's most agreeable neighborhoods, including Shepherd Park, the leafy area between 16th Street and Georgia Avenue, and Palisades, whose main street, MacArthur Boulevard, parallels the Potomac River. In Cleveland Park, an early twentieth-century enclave near the cathedral, media figures, senators, and lawyers live in spacious Victorian houses; their cars sport bumper stickers urging SAVE THE WHALES or even (says a reliable Washington source) DUKAKIS FOR PRESIDENT.

Upper Northwest is also home to off-the-beaten-path treasures like Rock Creek Park, the U.S. Soldiers and Airmen's Home, and the Kreeger Museum. Since this sprawling area is not all that well served by Metrorail, you'll need to take the city's Metrobus system to some of the places you want to go. In view of the distances involved, taxis or your own car are good alternatives for getting around.

The **Washington National Cathedral** or, more formally, The Cathedral Church of St. Peter and St. Paul, is far from being an off-the-beaten-path location. Every year 800,000 visitors go to Washington's highest point to explore one of America's great churches, a magnificent fourteenth-century-style cathedral begun when Teddy Roosevelt laid the cornerstone in 1907; it was completed in 1990. It would take a book like this just to adequately cover the cathedral's architectural detail and its highlights, including the exquisite stone carvings. For information about joining one of the regularly scheduled tours or attending any of the cathedral's vast array of musical events, special programs, and observances, call 537–6200 or visit www.cathedral.org. The cathedral is best reached by bus, using one of the "30" series lines north from Georgetown and downtown or by taking the Metro to the Tenleytown station (red line) and taking one of the 30 buses south about $1\frac{1}{2}$ miles to the cathedral.

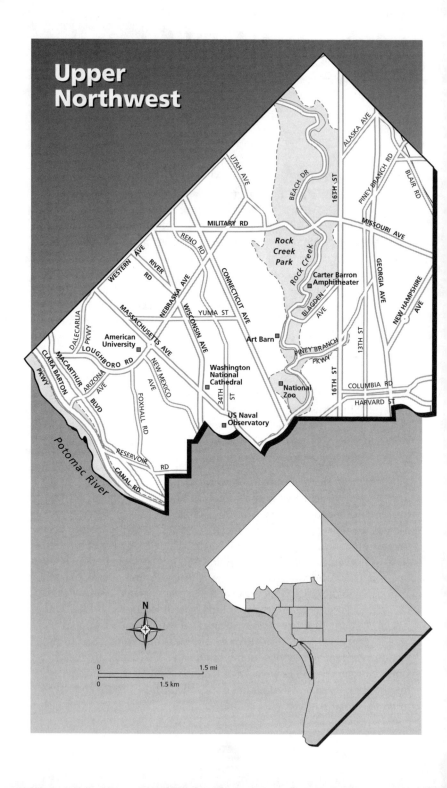

Upper
Northwest

UPPER NORTHWEST

TOP ATTRACTIONS IN UPPER NORTHWEST

National Cathedral

Rock Creek Park

Hillwood Museum

Kreeger Museum

U.S. Soldiers and Airmen's Home

Naval Observatory

While you're on the cathedral's sprawling fifty-seven-acre close, there are several eminently visitable places that are definitely off-the-beaten-path and are not to be missed. To see them, walk down South Road, to the right of the main doors, and walk down to the ***Herb Cottage.*** The cottage was once the Cathedral baptistry, but today it's one of Washington's top gift shops, with a nice selection of decorative china and porcelain, colorful trays and teapots, and nifty flowerpots, along with the obligatory jams and scents. There's a great selection of herbs too. The cottage is open daily 10:00 A.M. to 5:00 P.M. Call 537–8982.

Farther down South Road, an elaborately carved arch leads to the ***Bishop's Garden,*** which was conceived as a medieval walled garden of natural and ageless beauty to accompany a great Gothic cathedral. And that's exactly what it is. The garden is a collection of plants from historic gardens owned by Washington and Jefferson, while the "Hortulus" or "little garden" is planted with herbs found on a plant list created by Charlemagne in 815. The garden also includes ancient boxwoods, beds of fragrant herbs, and colorful seasonal blooms (hint: if it's tulips you're after, try April or May; roses appear in June). The garden's "Shadow House," a gazebo-like stone structure, makes a perfect spot to rest and reflect. During the growing season (April 1 to October 31)

Herb Cottage, Washington National Cathedral

Church Suppers

*B*ecause the Washington National Cathedral is in Cleveland Park, an overwhelmingly residential neighborhood, the selection of nearby restaurants is not large. However, the shopping area 2 blocks to the right as you exit the cathedral has two good choices:

• **Cafe Deluxe,** 3228 Wisconsin Avenue NW; 686–2233. Every neighborhood should have a restaurant this good. The Deluxe will remind you of a bright and bustling French cafe, but the food is largely American: burgers, great sandwiches, and the zenith of American comfort food, a top-notch meat loaf. Other favorites include pastas, grilled fish, and excellent desserts. There's also sidewalk dining in good weather, but the restaurant takes no reservations. Open Monday through Saturday 11:30 A.M. to 10:30 P.M.,

Sunday 11:00 A.M. to 10:00 P.M. Moderate.

• **Cactus Cantina,** 3300 Wisconsin Avenue NW; 686–7222. The Washingtonian's *estimable food critics recently called the Cactus Cantina one of the best restaurants in Upper Northwest, and they're absolutely right. This is the place to go for high quality Tex-Mex, especially the fajitas, grilled shrimp, and fat tamales. Believe it or not, the Cantina also has a "Cowboy and Indian Museum." So if you happen across a collection of cowboy hats, a Sioux "puberty bag," a figure of Chief Split Horn, and other Western curiosities, you'll know that it's not those eight or ten margaritas you ran through before dinner. Open Monday through Friday 11:30 A.M. to 11:00 P.M., weekends 11:30 A.M. to midnight. Sunday brunch is served from 11:30 A.M. to 3:00 P.M. Inexpensive.*

guided walk-in tours of the garden leave from the Herb Cottage every Wednesday at 10:30 A.M. Group tours can also be arranged by calling 244–0568. To learn about the program of special events in the garden, call 537–2937.

Below the Bishop's Garden, behind the equestrian statue of Washington, is **Olmsted Woods,** five acres of peaceful urban forest with footpaths great for taking a quiet walk among the black squirrels and songbirds. The woods are an ongoing effort by the Cathedral's All Hallows Guild to restore this oak and beech woodlands to its original pristine condition. The statue of Washington is more than just decoration; in the late eighteenth century these forests are where the first President used to ride horseback. Guided walks in the woods are given one Wednesday a month at 10:00 A.M. and leave from the Washington statue. Call 537–6282 to get the exact dates.

Refreshed and back on South Road, you're perfectly positioned for a shopping excursion in the cathedral's **Museum Store,** a cavernous and eclectic collection of everything from books and CDs with religious and secular themes to guidebooks and reproductions of the cathedral's gargoyles, grotesques, and other carvings. Definitely off-the-beaten-path is the store's stealth snack bar; it's along the shop's south wall. Open daily 9:30 A.M. to 5:30 P.M. Call 537–6267.

Farther down South Road are the **Cathedral Greenhouses,** which grow and sell hundreds of varieties of live herbs, annuals, and perennials. Even if you're not buying, it's fun to walk around, see the plants, and chat up the young employees who obviously love their work and the flowers. The greenhouse also has occasional special programs, including workshops, lectures, and children's events. For more information about them, call 537–6263. Open Monday through Saturday 9:00 A.M. to 6:00 P.M., Sunday 10:00 A.M. to 6:00 P.M.

One of the city's least-known treats for kids is the cathedral's hands-on **Medieval Workshop,** where children don aprons and gather around work benches to engage in supervised medieval crafts like molding gargolyes in clay, piecing together stained glass windows, and making brass rubbings. The workshops are held Saturdays from 10:00 A.M. to 2:00 P.M.; in July they are also offered Monday through Friday 1:00 to 4:00 P.M. No reservations are needed for groups of fewer than ten, just show up with your tots at the cathedral's crypt level. The charge is $4.00 per participant.

Another off-the-beaten-path possibility is the **Gargoyle Tour,** which combines a slide lecture with a close-up visit to some of those 107 often funny little carvings made by Italian craftsmen that parade around the cathedral's exterior, concealing waterspouts as they go. The tour costs $5.00. Reservations are needed; to make yours, call 537–2934.

Most people are so charmed by the cathedral and the lovely enclave that surrounds it that they'd like to stay on. With a little luck, that just might be possible. The **College of Preachers,** on the grounds at the rear of the cathedral, mainly offers rooms and conference space to church leaders and other individuals attending retreats, meetings, and other events at the cathedral, but opens its rooms to the public on a "space available" basis. It's a lovely experience. The college's Tudor-era building makes every visit feel something like a stay with Henry VIII, especially in the refectory, where the long tables, beamed walls and ceilings, and fabulous stained glass windows would make His Majesty (or Charles Laughton) feel right at home.

Nearby there's a quiet, book-filled library and a cloistered garden with fountain. The rooms, most with shared bath, are bright and comfortable. The College of Preachers is located at 3510 Woodley Road NW. Call 537–6383, fax 537–5650, or e-mail kgilliam@cathedral.org.

Not far from the back of the cathedral grounds is the *Vice President's House.* The best way to see what the Secret Service will allow is to stand at the corner of Massachusetts Avenue and 34th Street. Here you can gaze upon the massive white 1893 Queen Anne mansion that was once the home of the superintendent of the Naval Observatory, located next door, and, after that, "Quarters A," the residence of the Chief of Naval Operations, the Navy's top officer. But since 1974, this has been the official residence of the vice president. If you're not invited in, rest assured that it's spacious, comfortable, and just the place you'd want to live when *you* become vice president. Until then, keep standing on that corner.

One of the most fascinating but least known off-the-beaten-path excursions in Washington is the nighttime tour of the *U.S. Naval Observatory,* which is strictly off-limits to the public except on Monday evenings, when it opens its gates to outsiders. The observatory is the nation's main celestial tracker, supplier of astronomical data, and keeper of the United States Master Clock. The observatory's sensitive data is essential for accurate navigation and support of communications on earth and in space, so don't touch anything on your tour!

The tour includes a show-and-tell about the Master Clock and discussions with staff astronomers. Best of all, you'll be able to gaze skyward through the great 26-inch telescope that was used in the discovery in 1877 of the two moons of Mars. If the night sky is clear, you'll be invited to look through the historic 12-inch refracting telescope built in 1892. You will not, however, be invited to turn those lenses on the vice president and his family, who live in the big house next door.

The *U.S. Naval Observatory* is at Massachusetts Avenue at 34th Street NW; 762–1467, www.usno.navy.mil. Tours leave from the South Gate (on Observatory Circle opposite the New Zealand Embassy) every Monday at 8:30 P.M. Because only the first ninety people to appear are admitted and group tours are fairly common, walk-up guests should be at the gate by 7:30. The tour lasts ninety minutes. You'll be walking outside at night, and sometimes over rough ground, so consider bringing along a small flashlight and walking shoes. No Metro.

Farther out Wisconsin Avenue (take one of the "30" buses from the cathedral) is the place to visit if you're looking for a map to chart your hike across New Guinea, or some ideas for your next safari along Namibia's Skeleton Coast. Rochelle Jaffe's *Travel Books and Language Center* is travel central for Washington and probably the whole United States—a huge travel book store offering the country's largest collection of guides and literature. Aside from its planetwide selection of books, the store also has an extensive language center that includes phrase books, dictionaries, and serious study programs for every language you've ever heard of, from Guarani to Serbo-Croat.

Travel Books hosts an intensive schedule of special events, including regular book signings and lectures on everything from archaeological tours of Jordan to the Mustang Region of Nepal. Ms. Jaffe's monthly travel bulletins also include news of local language courses and travel book discussion groups. Travel Books and Language Center, 4437 Wisconsin Avenue NW (237–1322 or 800–220–2665, www.travelbks.com), is open Monday through Saturday 10:00 A.M. to 10:00 P.M., Sunday noon to 7:00 P.M. E-mail: travelbks@aol.com. Metro's Tenleytown (red line) station is a few steps away.

Close to the point where Wisconsin Avenue leaves the District for Maryland is the *Washington Dolls' House and Toy Museum,* a big favorite of local children and well worth a look for families with kids visiting the capital.

The Dolls' House Museum is a world-class collection of antique dolls' houses, toys, and games, mainly from the Victorian age. Of the dolls' houses, the most popular seem to be the model of an elegant 1890 mansion and a replica of a 1903 New Jersey seaside hotel. At the museum you'll also find a 1910 toy tableau of Teddy Roosevelt on safari and miniatures of German kitchens. There are rare toys that move when you wind them up or turn their handle, like the windup party with a piano player that pounds away while the ladies raise their cups. Speaking of tea, you can arrange children's birthdays and other parties in the museum's Edwardian Tea Room by reserving at 363–6400.

The museum has an extensive shop of dollhouse furniture and dolls, along with a Consignment Corner selling antique dolls and toys. Admission: $4.00 for adults, $3.00 for seniors, $2.00 for children under twelve. The Washington Dolls' House and Toy Museum, 5236 44th Street NW, is open Tuesday through Saturday 10:00 A.M. to 5:00 P.M. Sunday noon to 5:00 P.M. Metro: Friendship Heights (red line).

Incidentally, the museum is in the midst of one of Washington's primo shopping areas. Lord & Taylor is around the corner, and both the huge

Mazza Gallery across the street and the Chevy Chase Pavilion across Wisconsin Avenue contain big-name stores like Nieman Marcus that will really melt your plastic. The area also offers a wide assortment of eateries. If that isn't enough, the shopping doesn't stop there, but continues northward up Wisconsin Avenue and into Chevy Chase, Maryland, in a strip that includes Tiffany's, Saks Fifth Avenue, and Brooks Brothers.

The little red schoolhouse on MacArthur Boulevard, not far from the Potomac, was built in 1864, making it the oldest one-room schoolhouse in the District. Now it's the home of **Discovery Creek,** a children's museum and activity center designed to help kids, especially ages four to eleven, experience and respect the natural environment. The museum is lined with terraria containing lizards and reptiles, plus other exhibits where kids can learn about wildlife and nature. Using the school as a base, Discovery Creek sponsors an extensive year-round program of outdoor adventures and other science- or nature-oriented programs either in the schoolhouse or at other area locations. The school is located on the edge of Palisades Park, which makes nature hikes and other big-league explorations a breeze. Discovery Creek, the Children's Museum of Washington, is at 4954 MacArthur Boulevard NW. Call 364–3111, fax 364–3114, or visit www.discoverycreek.org.

A short walk from Discovery Creek, just up Chain Bridge Road from the intersection with MacArthur Boulevard, you'll find one of the District's least known and most touching places, **The Union Burial Society of Georgetown Cemetery,** a two-acre burial ground for former slaves and their descendants at 2616 Chain Bridge Road. Except for the community's former schoolhouse, which still stands at 2820 Chain Bridge Road (not open to the public), this 200-year-old cemetery is almost the last vestige of a small black settlement that inhabited the residential area now known as the Palisades. It is well cared for by a descendant of one of the families buried there. The cemetery is usually open during the day, but has no fixed hours.

Despite its current tranquillity and affluence, Chain Bridge Road was, in the eighteenth and nineteenth centuries, a busy and much traveled highway leading to Chain Bridge, one of the earliest (and still standing) bridges across the Potomac. If you go a little farther up this sunken road you'll arrive at **Battery Kemble Fort,** very agreeable for walks and picnics. Although it is now a totally suburbanized city park, Battery Kemble was once a keystone of the "circle of forts" that defended the District during the Civil War. You'll also gaze upon the houses of the rich and famous that line Chain Bridge Road, which is now one of Washington's very best addresses.

The *Kreeger Museum* displays the art and sculpture collection of David Lloyd Kreeger, insurance mogul, philanthropist, and art collector extra-ordinaire, in an intimate atmosphere. In fact, just a glance at the museum itself, a 1967 design by famed architect Philip Johnson, tells visitors that they have arrived at a special place. To get the idea, imagine an architectural wedding of classical and Renaissance—a sprawling Roman villa in white travertine with soaring neo-Palladian windows that expose its exhibit walls to warmth and sunlight.

The two-story atrium of the museum's Great Hall showcases impression-ist masterpieces including Picassos and van Goghs, while the Kreeger's former dining room now serves up a feast of Monets. Across the atrium, Mondrian's *Mill on the River* presides over a teak-lined library.

The Kreeger's downstairs rooms lack the spacious feel of the Great Hall, but compensate with more Picassos, Miro etchings, a Frank Stella, and works by other abstract expressionists. Somewhat incongruously, there's also a fascinating collection of African wood carvings and tribal masks. The Kreeger Museum, at 2401 Foxhall Road (337–3050, fax 337–3051), hosts conducted, ninety-minute tours twice a day, at 10:30 A.M. and 1:30 P.M. Tuesday through Saturday, but is closed the month of August. Children under twelve are not admitted. Reservations are essential and should be obtained well in advance by calling (202) 338–3552 or visiting www.kreegermuseum.com on-line. Suggested donation is $5.00. Because the Kreeger is far from public transporta-tion, a personal vehicle or taxi is best.

As Truman Capote said about Venice, a visit to *Hillwood* is a great treat, "like eating an entire box of chocolate liqueurs all at one go." This forty-room mansion of cereal heiress Marjorie Merriweather Post is one superlative after another, especially when describing its wealth of Russ-ian decorative art, a collection that began when one of Mrs. Post's four husbands, Joseph E. Davies, served as the American ambassador to Moscow in the late '30s. Among Hillwood's riches, the high point is the Icon Room, which gleams with enamel and gold Fabergé eggs and clocks, a dazzling diamond tiara worn by the last empress, and masses of jewel-encrusted gold and silver chalices. The Russian porcelain room is special too, chiefly for the four dinner services that once belonged to Catherine the Great and some pieces from the personal dinner service of Empress Elizabeth I made in the late 1750s.

Hillwood's Russian art is rivaled only by its array of French antiques. A portrait of Empress Eugenie and hangings of Gobelin tapestries look down on Hillwood's French drawing room, where the wood paneling

OFF THE BEATEN PATH

Capital Quote

"Rock Creek has an abundance of all the elements that make up not only pleasing, but wild and rugged scenery. There is, perhaps, not another city in the Union that has on its very threshold so much natural beauty and grandeur."

—Naturalist and author
John Burroughs

comes from a French château and the rolltop Roentgen desk is a marvel of marquetry. In the dining room Mrs. Post's guests banqueted by the light of Russian Imperial candlesticks on Russian Imperial porcelain; the room's Aubusson carpet once belonged to the Emperor Maximilian. After exploring Hillwood, don't forget to saunter through the estate's formal gardens and look in on the excellent collection of native American arts gathered in the Adirondack Building. Docent-led and audio-guided tours of Hillwood Museum, at 4155 Linnean Avenue NW, are given five times daily on Tuesday through Saturday between 9:00 A.M. and 5:00 P.M. Closed in February. Call 686–5807 for the necessary reservations. Suggested donation is $10. Minimum visitor age in the house is six. Hillwood's Cafe offers terrific food and an afternoon tea; reserve for lunch at 686–8505, ext. 8517. Hillwood is about 1 mile from the Van Ness Metro station (red line) and from all Connecticut Avenue bus routes.

Rock Creek Park is one of America's oldest, largest, and most beautiful urban parks and one of Washington's great treasures. This wedge-shaped, 2,800-acre wilderness follows Rock Creek, a rushing rural stream, for 6 often secluded miles right through the heart of a busy city, starting at the Kennedy Center and ending at the District's border with Maryland, passing the National Zoo as it winds along. And unlike New York's Central Park, Rock Creek is hilly, a gorge with ravines and hidden pockets of heavily wooded forests and running brooks. It's so nice that, after the Civil War, a commission formed to find a "healthier situation" for a new Executive Mansion to replace the White House gave this in-town oasis serious consideration.

Rock Creek was made a national park in 1890 when Congress set it aside as "a pleasuring place for the enjoyment of the people of the United States"; ever since, Washingtonians have happily headed there to bicycle, walk its 29 miles of foot trails, ride the 13 miles of bridle paths, and even play golf. Picnicking too—within this city forest there are dozens of clearings with picnic tables that during the spring and summer are the scenes of family gatherings and softball games. Picnicking in some areas requires permission; call 673–7646 about permits. Presidents also have been big Rock Creek fans, including Teddy Roosevelt, who loved the park and hiked there often, and Ronald Reagan, who often rode at the stables. The Park Service Web site for Rock Creek is www.nps.gov/rocr.

French Bench

*J*ules Jusserand may not be a house-hold name today, but if you'd lived in Washington any time between 1902 and 1925, when Jusserand was the French Ambassador to the United States, you'd certainly have heard about him.

One reason Monsieur Jusserand stayed in Washington for twenty-three years was his ability to befriend every U.S. President he ever met, from Teddy Roosevelt to Warren Harding; he was influential in persuading Woodrow Wilson that the United States should join the Allied side in World War I. What's more, Jusserand was also a noted scholar; his book, With Americans of Past and Present Days, won the 1917 Pulitzer Prize for U.S. history.

Jusserand and Teddy Roosevelt were great bird-watchers and frequently went birding together in Rock Creek Park. Jusserand is remembered today with a stone bench in the park, in the woods across Rock Creek from Pierce Mill.

The park remains a hidden corner for many visitors without their own automobiles, in part because there are no metro stations in the park and no buses roll along Rock Creek Parkway and Beach Drive, its two main thoroughfares. Nevertheless, it's not all that difficult to enjoy the park and its excellent facilities.

One way is to start at the corner of Rock Creek Parkway and Virginia Avenue NW across from the Watergate, and simply follow the path next to the parkway back into the park. Along the way you'll pass under Embassy Row and behind the zoo before you reach Tilden Street, where the park's most scenic area begins with Pierce Mill.

Another way of getting to Pierce Mill involves taking the Metro's red line to the Cleveland Park station, then walking up Connecticut Avenue 2 blocks north to Rodman Street; at the corner you'll see an inviting little woods with signs directing you down the Melvin Hazen Trail. The trail leads a short distance down to Rock Creek where a left (north) turn on West Ridge Trail takes you, after a few minutes, to the mill.

Pierce Mill, named for the family that built and ran the mill in the early nineteenth century, was one of eight mills that lined Rock Creek in the 1820s and used its waterpower to grind corn and wheat into flour. The mill outlived its economic usefulness and was closed in 1897. But today this lovely stone building, with its wooden waterwheel, is once again a functioning flour mill with antique millstones and hoppers that give visitors a fascinating view of a functioning nineteenth-century flour and cornmeal mill. Pierce Mill, at the intersection of Beach Drive and

Pierce Mill, Rock Creek Park

Tilden Street NW, is open Wednesday through Sunday noon to 5:00 P.M. Call 426–6908. Contributions are welcome.

Next door to the mill is the trim little "Art Barn," built in 1820 as the Pierce family's carriage house. The barn now hosts the **Rock Creek Gallery,** an art gallery with a series of eleven rotating monthly exhibits by local artists along with special art programs. The Gallery also offers a children's summer camp and art workshops, and poetry readings at 8:00 P.M. every Thursday. Open Thursday through Sunday noon to 6:00 P.M. The gallery is sometimes closed in July, so if that's when you're going, you'd better check first at 244–2482.

If you're on foot, at Pierce Mill you have the option of following markers along West Ridge Trail 1^1/$_2$ miles south to the National Zoo and its Metro stop on the red line or 2 miles north to the Park's **Nature Center.**

The Nature Center is the hub of Park Service programs and activities in the park, and there are a lot of them. To get an idea of the range of flora and fauna that live here in the middle of a large city, wander through the displays, photographs, and explanatory data in the center's large exhibit area. The center also has a bevy of children's programs, including a special "discovery room" for those under eight. As the park's "information central," the center can supply checklists of birds to watch for, a road map of the bike and other trails that crisscross the park, and instructions on a self-guided walk along the Nature Center Trail, where you can see firsthand most of the plants, birds, and animals you saw mounted back at the center. The center also offers guided nature walks and a small bookshop with a well-chosen selection of publications on natural history.

Perhaps the most remarkable section of the center is its seventy-five-seat planetarium, the only one in the Park Service system, which offers regularly scheduled events that acquaint children with the elements of astronomy and relate ancient yarns about the influence of the stars and moon. Planetarium shows are given on Wednesday at 4:00 P.M. and on Saturday and Sunday at 1:00 and 4:00 P.M. The Nature Center, 5200 Glover Road NW (426–6829), is open Wednesday through Sunday 9:00 A.M. to 5:00 P.M. You can either drive to the center by following the directional signs from nearby Military Road, or take the Metro to the Friendship Heights station (red line) then transfer to an E2 or E3 bus to the corner of Oregon Avenue and Military Road, at which point you're a short walk from the center. If you decide to drive, keep in mind that Beach Drive is closed to auto traffic from 7:00 A.M. Saturday to 7:00 P.M. Sunday.

The *Rock Creek Park Horse Center,* run by a concessionaire, is a short walk from the Nature Center. This is where you can either visit the horses or arrange to ride one and become a true urban cowboy. The Horse Center has large indoor and outdoor rings and offers a variety of riding programs, including pony rides on weekends and by appointment for $7.50 for fifteen minutes. If you're interested in trail rides, one-hour rides are given Tuesday, Wednesday, and Thursday at 3:00 P.M. and Saturday and Sunday at noon, 1:30 and 3:00 P.M. at a cost of $25. The Horse Center's office is open Tuesday through Friday 2:00 to 8:00 P.M. and Saturday and Sunday 10:00 A.M. to 5:00 P.M. Call 362–0118.

Despite its daytime glories, you'd be well advised not to walk in this park after nightfall.

The Club Bus

*T*he Metro folks have added a new bus service that will help you get from Upper Northwest into the nightlife in other neighborhoods. Route 98, the Adams Morgan–U Street Link, runs between the Woodley Park Zoo/Adams Morgan Metro station and 18th Street, the heart of Adams Morgan; it then continues on to Shaw's U Street/Cardozo Metro station. The service runs every fifteen minutes between 6:00 P.M. and midnight Sunday through Thursday, 6:00 P.M. to 1:00 A.M. on Friday, and 10:00 A.M. to 1:00 A.M. on Saturday. Fare is $1.10, but with a transfer ticket from Metrorail, it's only a quarter.

If, after your visit to Rock Creek Park, the idea of hiking some of Washington's other trails is appealing, you've got some great walks in store. For an excellent map and overview of what else is available in the District, visit www.washdc.org/trail.html.

Not far from the Nature Center, you'll see the place where, in July 1864, Confederate forces led by General Jubal Early made their first and last attempt to seize Washington with a bold attack on the Union defenses that surrounded the capital. Early's 20,000 troops launched their assault by marching down the Seventh Street Road, today's Georgia Avenue, from Silver Spring, Maryland, now a Washington suburb. The Confederate forces were met and repelled at **Fort Stevens,** another one of the "circle of forts" that protected the capital in wartime, whose commander, Gen. Lew Wallace, would go on to make Charlton Heston famous by writing *Ben Hur.*

Abraham Lincoln visited Fort Stevens during the fighting and even mounted the ramparts to check out the action, exposing his lanky figure to enemy fire. When a young Union officer, said to be future Chief Justice Oliver Wendell Holmes, spotted a tall civilian peering over at the rebel forces, he shouted, "Get down, you damned fool!" Lincoln complied. The spot is marked by a boulder and plaque. You can easily visit Fort Stevens (www.nps.gov/cwdw/stevens), now a grassy park at the corner of 13th Street and Quackenbos Road NW, just off Georgia Avenue; the fort has been partially reconstructed, with its original earthworks and cannon standing ready in their emplacements and pointing north toward the Confederate lines. To reach the fort, take the Metro to Silver Spring (red line), then the 70 or 71 bus to Quackenbos Street.

Nearby, at 6625 Georgia Avenue NW, is **Battleground National Cemetery** (www.nps.gov/cwdw/btcemet.htm), where forty-one of the

Glover Archbold Park

*T*his slender, 3-mile-long, 183-acre park runs through some of northwest Washington's best neighborhoods and most secluded woodlands. Although it is less well known and smaller than Rock Creek Park, it also makes a great place for an urban ramble or jog.

To reach Glover Archbold, take the Metro's red line to Tenleytown, then walk south several blocks on Wisconsin Avenue to Van Ness Street. A right turn will take you 1 block to a grassy park on the left where a sign marks the northern end of the park. The trail ends at a stone tunnel under the C&O Canal (one of the canal's original structures), which opens on to the canal towpath about a ten-minute walk from Georgetown.

soldiers killed in the defense of Fort Stevens are buried. This poignant, rarely visited plot is the nation's smallest national cemetery. The cannon at the entrance gate are from Fort Stevens and were used in the Civil War battle. Inside, monuments commemorate the fallen of the 122nd New York Volunteers and other regiments; in the rear a flagpole is surrounded by a circle of headstones. Open dawn to dusk. You can visit the cemetery by taking the Metro red line to Silver Spring, then transferring to the 70 or 71 bus line and getting off at Aspen Street.

The *National Museum of Health and Medicine* charts the progress of medicine over the centuries, and many of its exhibits focus on pathology, the history of disease, and the development of human life. The museum also has the world's largest collection of microscopes and an internationally renowned neuroanatomical collection (read brain specimens).

The museum's visual centerpieces, however, are the exhibits of U.S. military medicine in wartime. The most extensive and interesting of these are those covering Civil War medicine, which contain some very graphic photos and wax reproductions of grievous wounds and smashed bones. Another set of models and photographs shows the reconstructive surgery used at the time to repair shattered faces and limbs and the techniques battlefield doctors used for amputations and in dealing with trauma. The museum also has casts of Lincoln's face and hands and the actual bullet that killed the President at Ford's Theater.

After the Civil War, it's on to a medical tour of Korea's MASH units and World War II, which includes an unforgettable display of the Army's fight against VD, with some photos of afflicted GIs that will definitely make you think more than twice before ever fooling around.

The National Museum of Health and Medicine is located in building 54 on the campus of Walter Reed Hospital at 6900 Georgia Avenue NW; 782–2200, www.natmedmuse.afip.org. Open daily 10:00 A.M. to 5:30 P.M. Take the 70 or 71 bus south from the Silver Spring Metro station (red line).

Faced with the blazing heat and swampy moisture of a non-air-conditioned Washington summer, Abraham and Mary Lincoln would drive out Seventh Street NW to stay in the cool and spacious grounds of the *U.S. Soldier's Home* in the rural expanses of northwest Washington, making the home the first presidential Camp David.

The home was established for aging and ailing soldiers in 1851 and it is still a retirement home for 1,100 soldiers and airmen. One of its main buildings, *Anderson Cottage,* a fourteen-room Victorian Gothic house, was originally built as a summer retreat by a wealthy banker, then made available to presidents when it was no longer needed for veterans.

Historians estimate that Lincoln spent about one-fourth of his administration living in Anderson Cottage. It was there he signed the Emancipation Proclamation, conferred with his generals, and spent time with his family, especially young Tad, with whom he often climbed the sprawling 300-year-old copper beech tree that still stands next to the cottage. Lincoln last visited the cottage on April 13, 1865, the day before he was assassinated, to make sure it was ready for his family's next summer visit.

Although the Soldier's Home grounds were an inviting refuge from tropical Washington, Anderson House has long attracted the attention of Lincoln scholars and historians. The house is still attractive, intact, and structurally sound—in many ways a time capsule where you can walk the porch where Lincoln reflected and peer through the windows at the rooms and fireplace he knew well. But you can't count on being able to go in, because the house now holds the offices of a veteran's retirement center and is usually not open to visitors. However, exceptions are sometimes made (see below).

In mid-2000 this little-known but historically significant house was placed at the top of the National Trust for Historic Preservation's list of endangered places needing urgent attention, which in the case of Anderson means arresting water seepage and deteriorating woodwork. According to the trust's president, "it's probably the country's most significant Lincoln site because it is the only one associated with his presidency, and the only major Lincoln site that has not been restored." One possible use being discussed for a restored cottage is as a study center for Lincoln scholars. Just for the record, the cottage was used by three other Presidents as their summer White House: Lincoln's predecessor, James Buchanan, then Rutherford B. Hayes (1877–80) and Chester Alan Arthur (1882–84).

The gates of the U.S. Soldiers and Airmen's Home, at Rock Creek Church Road and Upshur Street NW and at 3700 North Capitol Street NW, are open from 7:00 A.M. to 4:00 P.M. Because this is a facility primarily to care for military retirees, admission to the grounds and the Anderson Cottage is regulated and sometimes denied. By calling 730–3337, you can arrange one of the cottage tours, which are given only on Thursday and Friday. To enter the grounds to see the cottage exterior, you'll need prior authorization, which you can request by calling ahead, 730–3337. Take along a picture ID. There is no direct Metro service, but the 60 bus from the Ft. Totten Metro station (red and green lines) will take you to the Upshur Street gate. Best of all: Drive or cab it.

If you have time, visit the nearby *Soldier's Home National Cemetery,* the entrance of which is at the corner of Rock Creek Church Road and Harewood Road. It was among the first to be established to hold the remains of Civil War dead and predates Arlington National Cemetery, which was created, in part, because this cemetery was filled.

If you go to the Soldier's Home you'll have both the pleasure of visiting the Lincoln Cottage, one of America's seldom visited historical treasures, and dining at the down-home *Hitching Post,* another off-the-beaten-path find that is also unknown even to Washingtonians. Located just opposite the Soldier's Home's gate on Rock Creek Church Road, the Hitching Post is the quintessential neighborhood restaurant, where you'll either perch on stools at the Formica counter or settle into one of four fuchsia-colored Naugahyde booths to enjoy terrific southern cooking. From their tiny kitchen, Adrienne and Alvin Carter will fix you the best southern fried chicken you've ever had, or enormous crab cakes, arguably the best in town, packed with moist crab meat, along with a side of great slaw. The menu also lists baked ham and lamb chops, which I'm saving for my next visit. The Hitching Post, 200 Upshur Street NW (726–1511), is open Tuesday through Saturday noon to midnight. Inexpensive to moderate.

PLACES TO STAY IN UPPER NORTHWEST

The Kalorama Guest House, 2700 Cathedral Avenue NW; 328–0860. This urban B&B consists of two handsome 1910–1912 town houses with nineteen agreeable rooms, seven of which involve shared bathrooms. And there's no beating the location, a nice residential neighborhood around the corner from the National Zoo and 2 blocks from the Metro. Inexpensive.

Savoy Suites, 2505 Wisconsin Avenue NW; 337–9700 or (800) 944–5377. This large (150 unit) suite hotel calls itself a Georgetown hotel, but it is in fact located close to the National Cathedral in Upper Northwest, a fifteen-minute walk from Georgetown. Some of its 150 comfortable suites have kitchens and many come with Jacuzzi tubs. The Savoy also has a bistro serving traditional Italian favorites. Moderate. No Metro, but on the route of the "30" buses.

Omni Shoreham, 2500 Calvert Street NW; 234–0700. This seventy-year-old Washington tradition with 812 rooms is hardly a cozy hideaway, but it sure offers a great travel experience, with top-drawer service and a historic feel. The Shoreham is like a small, self-contained city, with restaurants, shops, and a health club. Many rooms have superb views of Rock Creek Park.

The Shoreham is also handy to the Metro and the Zoo, and is only a short cab ride from Adams Morgan's lively restaurant scene. Expensive.

PLACES TO EAT IN UPPER NORTHWEST

Chef Geoff's, 3201 New Mexico Avenue NW; 237–7800, www.chefgeoff. com. This great American bistro is located in a tony neighborhood that needs all the restaurant help it can get. But Geoff would do well anywhere in the city with his "stone pies" (a.k.a. pizza), crab cakes, and grilled or seared fish entrees. The service is friendly, laid-back, and professional, and the wine list is both well chosen and well priced. Open daily 11:30 A.M. to 10:00 P.M. Sunday brunch starts at 11:00 A.M. Moderate.

Lavandou, 3321 Connecticut Avenue NW; 966–3002. If you dine here, you'll be joining the locals in one of their favorite places—one that they'd just as soon keep to themselves. Too bad for them, the word is out about Lavandou's pork

tenderloin, sea scallops in red wine sauce, and carbonnade, which are among the house specialties. Afterward, remember to call for the dessert cart and to forget the calories. The service and atmosphere are also very good. Lavandou is a 3-block walk from the National Zoo. Moderate.

Lebanese Taverna, 2641 Connecticut Avenue NW, located near the National Zoo; 265–8681. A great place to try *meze,* the Lebanese equivalent of tapas, or the flavorful kabobs and broiled chicken. Open daily 11:00 A.M. to 2:30 P.M., 5:30 to 10:30 P.M., until 11:00 on Friday and Saturday. Moderate. Across from Woodley Park–Zoo Metro station (red line).

Oxford Tavern, 3000 Connecticut Avenue NW; 232–4225. Better known as the "Zoo Bar," located just opposite the National Zoo entrance, the Oxford has a long menu of pizzas, burgers, sandwiches, and salads,

plus a kids menu. Open daily 10:00 A.M. to 11:00 P.M. For grown-ups there's also a lively bar and even livelier music Friday and Saturday 10:00 P.M. to 2:00 A.M. Inexpensive. Metro: Woodley Park–Zoo (red line).

Rocklands Barbecue and Grilling Company, 2418 Wisconsin Avenue NW; 333–2558. You'll get probably the best barbecue in the District in this modest storefront with a giant wood grill. Rocklands has a few stools for sit-down diners, but you can either eat your pork ribs or chicken standing in the corner next to the world-class collection of 120 spicy sauces and condiments or take them along on your walk through nearby Glover-Archbold Park. You can make a virtual visit at www.rocklands.com, but you won't get the great smell of that wood grill. Open Monday through Friday 11:30 A.M. to 10:00 P.M., Saturday 11:00 A.M. to 10:00 P.M., and Sunday 11:00 A.M. to 9:00 P.M. Inexpensive.

Where to Find the Author's Favorite Places to Stay in Upper Northwest

College of Preachers
3510 Woodley Road NW; 537–638
(see page 107 for full listing)

Saveur, 2218 Wisconsin Avenue NW; 333–5885, fax 333–1104. This storefront find between the National Cathedral and Georgetown has an eclectic and imaginative menu with risottos, rack of lamb, beef medallions, and crab cakes, but its real specialties are focused on game. Try the seared duck breast with duck sausage or a roast venison, maybe the best you'll ever eat, then follow up with a chocolate Wellington or another megacalorie dessert. Since chef Kao Koumtakoun frequently works the room to greet diners, you'll have a chance to tell him personally how great it is. Knowledgeable, friendly service, moderate prices, and a super-romantic atmosphere. No Metro, but the "30" buses will get you there. Expensive.

Where to Find the Author's Favorite Places to Eat in Upper Northwest

Cafe Deluxe
3228 Wisconsin Avenue NW; 686–2233
(see page 106 for full listing)

Cactus Cantina
3300 Wisconsin Avenue NW; 686–7222
(see page 106 for full listing)

Hitching Post
200 Upshur Street NW; 726–1511
(see page 119 for full listing)

Dupont Circle

Dupont Circle is probably Washington's liveliest neighborhood, with a raffish street life and an intellectual reputation fueled by plenty of first-rate bookstores and cafes, several of them catering to the area's large gay community. The Circle offers visitors an abundance of house museums, art galleries, and restaurants along with a laid-back lifestyle that makes casual strolling a joy. Although the present, in itself, would make Dupont Circle an agreeable place to hang out, this neighborhood's past gives it an extra dimension that enriches any visit.

At the turn of the twentieth century, Dupont Circle was called "Washington's Newport," one of America's most fashionable districts, where the nation's lumber barons, steel kings, and other merchant moguls built the hundreds of grand winter homes and town houses that continue to grace the area. Nowadays this neighborhood and its brownstone town houses, redbrick turrets, and Beaux Arts palaces includes the Massachusetts Avenue corridor called Embassy Row, which bristles with the flags of many nations not even dreamed of during its Victorian heyday. Behind the opulent mansions that line Massachusetts Avenue, quiet streets filter back into Kalorama, a residential neighborhood that has known elegant living in three centuries.

The Dupont Circle stop on the Metro's red line serves most of the sites in this chapter. Dupont Circle itself is named not for a member of the great chemical family, but after Samuel Francis Dupont, an admiral in the Union Navy. A large fountain commemorating his exploits sits in the center of the Circle, which is actually a small oasis at the intersection of three main streets: New Hampshire, Massachusetts, and Connecticut Avenues. Despite the constant traffic, the Circle has a small-town feel, with plenty of benches for checkers and conversation.

In 1892, when millionaire brewer Christian Heurich (pronounced *hy-rick*) built his thirty-one-room dream castle on New Hampshire Avenue just off the Circle, many of the other mansions that ringed Dupont Circle were built by newly minted industrial titans eager to forget their humble or distant origins. Not Heurich, who wanted his home to celebrate his

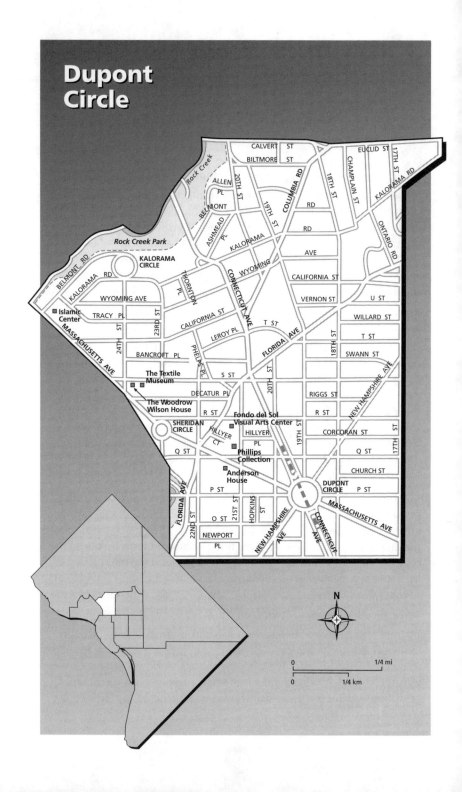

Dupont Circle

TOP ATTRACTIONS IN DUPONT CIRCLE

Phillips Collection

Anderson House

The Heurich House Museum

The Textile Museum

The Woodrow Wilson House

The Lindens

German ancestry. The result is an unlikely marriage of Queen Victoria and Count von Bismarck, a ponderous brownstone home in Romanesque Revival style (or as one observer put it, "beer barrel baronial") with high-ceilinged rooms where William McKinley would feel right at home.

At the **Heurich House Museum,** you'll see the meaning of ornate, from the parlor brimming with objets d'art, to the music room with its musician's gallery, to the majestic dining room in carved walnut, with a table elaborately set for eighteen. Amid all this Gilded Age splendor you'll find German mythological scenes elaborately carved by craftsmen on the furniture, wainscoting, and the house's seventeen marble fireplaces. If the public rooms become a little too formal, lighten up by heading downstairs to the basement breakfast room, which doubled as the family *bierstube.* Here the Heurichs gathered for family meals and steins of the family product surrounded by mottoes (in German, of course) celebrating the pleasures of the glass. Since Heurich lived to be 102, maybe the suggestion that "A good drink rejuvenates" isn't such bad advice. The mansion is now the headquarters of the Historical Society of Washington, which maintains a reference library and museum shop there. The handsome little garden behind the house is perfect for a picnic or a rest. The Heurich House Museum, 1307 New Hampshire Avenue NW (785–2068), is open Wednesday through Saturday 10:00 A.M. to 4:00 P.M. Admission is $3.00.

Your vote for most beautiful shop in D.C. might go to **Marston Luce,** an out-of-the-way storefront luminous with eighteenth- and nineteenth-century French antiques, especially pine armoires and tables. This citadel of exquisite taste will also gladly sell you a nice Provençal buffet, a lovely flowered screen from Louis Napoleon's Paris, or a peaceful French landscape. As a nice touch for your garden, snap up that bucket of vintage pétanque balls so you'll be the first in your neighborhood to lawn bowl, French style. Expensive, but lots cheaper than a trip to France. Marston Luce, at 1314 21st Street NW (775–9460. www.marstonluce.com), is open Monday through Saturday 11:00 A.M. to 6:00 P.M.

Yes, it's true—at the **Brickskeller** you can get terrific burgers and good buffalo steaks from the Dakotas, not to mention some nice rainbow trout. But the big attraction is the Brickskeller's world-class collection of beers, totaling more than 900 brands at last count (that is, if you're sober enough to count). There are a lot of saloons in this country that make a big deal of their collection of microbrews and exotic foreign labels, but nobody, repeat nobody, beats the Brickskeller. For proof, just check out the house collection of empties that lines the walls of this restaurant, elegantly decorated in Early American Fraternity House style. No wine list to worry about here. To spare yourself the embarrassment of ordering the wrong beer with pierogies, just ask your knowledgeable sommelier of suds to bring over the Brickskeller's book of brews for a consultation. (Hint: A young, presumptuous, and slightly spritzy San Miguel—a late harvest '97—would be perfect). The Brickskeller is located at 1523 22nd Street NW; 293–1885. Open Monday through Friday 11:30 A.M. to 2:00 A.M., Saturday 6:00 P.M. to 3:00 A.M., and Sunday 6:00 P.M. to 2:00 A.M. Inexpensive—if you shop after only one beer.

None of Massachusetts Avenue's great mansions reflects power and wealth more than **Anderson House,** whose massive facade fairly oozes authority. Now the headquarters of the Society of the Cincinnati, a venerable organization of Revolutionary War descendants, Anderson House was for many years the home of wealthy career diplomat Larz Anderson. In keeping with the "Washington's Newport" reputation of this neighborhood, the Andersons used this colossal house for only a few months every year.

Keep in mind that Anderson House suffers from a touch of schizophrenia. You'll start off on the ground floor with the Society's impressive collections of Revolutionary War memorabilia and paintings by John Trumbull, Gilbert Stuart, and other early American artists. But on the second floor, the Anderson House suddenly becomes a treasure trove of eclectic antiquities and furnishings that largely reflect Anderson's years in Europe and Asia as the American ambassador to Japan and Belgium. Several rooms hold rare Japanese and Chinese carvings and lacquers acquired during Anderson's years in Asia, while others are strictly European, including the highly traditional English parlor with

French Kosher Anyone?

*U*nless someone told you that *L'Etoile* is strictly kosher, you might never guess. The menu features familiar French bistro favorites like an authentic pâté (of beef, naturally), cassoulet, Moroccan lamb stew, and confit of duck, all carefully prepared to observe dietary laws. The wines are all kosher as well. Of course no dairy, no shellfish. L'Etoile, 1310 New Hampshire Avenue NW (835–3030), is open for lunch daily 11:30 A.M. to 2:00 P.M. and for dinner Sunday through Friday 5:30 to 10:00 P.M. Reservations by credit card required for Friday dinner and Saturday lunch. Moderate.

DUPONT CIRCLE

AUTHOR'S FAVORITES IN DUPONT CIRCLE

Phillips Collection

Second Story Books

Kramerbooks and Afterwords Cafe and Grill

Adams Morgan

Kalorama Walk

Embassy Row

Hepplewhite chairs and portraits by Reynolds and Hoppner.

What makes the very rich different from you and me becomes obvious in the Anderson's sumptuous dining room. You know you're not back home in your cozy breakfast nook when you see how the Andersons, even *à deux*, dined at a table for twenty-eight in a room graced with Carrara marble floors, seventeenth-century Belgian tapestries, and priceless Japanese screens. After dinner the ambassador and his wife led their guests downstairs to their vast ballroom, which conjures up visions of black-tie evenings in a long-vanished Washington. Outside the ballroom there's the garden and, in the center, a grand seventeenth-century Buddha. Amid this elegance and ostentation you'll find indications that this regal couple also had a nice sense of humor; in the solarium you'll see the amusing cartoon of the Andersons tooting along in their open touring car and a map tracing their favorite drives around Washington. Anderson House, at 2118 Massachusetts Avenue NW (785–2040), is open Tuesday through Saturday 1:00 to 4:00 P.M.

In the Phillips Mansion at Massachusetts Avenue and 21st Street, you'll find one of America's finest collections of modern art. Private at first, the *Phillips Collection* went public in 1921, when wealthy collector Duncan Phillips opened a few rooms of the family home to art lovers. The collection has since expanded to occupy the entire mansion and a recent annex.

The collection reflects Phillips's refined and diverse tastes, especially his love for the French Impressionists. Here, in an intimate and charming setting, you'll find Renoir's *Luncheon of the Boating Party* and other treasures such as Degas' *Dancers at the Bar* and masterpieces by Bonnard, Cézanne, Matisse, and Daumier. There are also important works by neoclassicists and realists such as Corot and Courbet along with American modernists Georgia O'Keeffe and Edward Hopper. As you wander through this explosion of great art, you'll also be able to inspect the public rooms of the Phillips mansion, including the grandiose Music Room, with its intricate Italianate ceiling. The Music Room is also the site of the collection's Sunday afternoon concerts, which are held at 5:00 P.M. September through May. The concerts are free with museum admission, but it's a good idea to arrive early. The Phillips Collection, 1600 21st Street NW (387–2151; www.phillipscollection.com), is open Tuesday, Wednesday, Friday, and Saturday 10:00 A.M. to 5:00 P.M., Sunday noon to 7:00 P.M.; closed Monday. On Thursday, when there's an "Artful Evenings" program of live jazz, lectures, and a cash bar, the hours are 10:00 A.M. to 8:30 P.M. Regular admission is $6.50; the charge for Artful Evenings is $7.50.

The Phillips also has an excellent gift shop open Tuesday through Saturday from 10:00 A.M. to 5:00 P.M. and Sunday from noon to 5:00 P.M. Closed Monday. Next to the gift shop, the Phillips Cafe serves coffee, light lunches, and soups Tuesday through Saturday 10:45 A.M. to 4:30 P.M. and on Sunday from noon to 4:30 P.M.

Back on 21st Street, a left turn leads to R Street and a handsome block lined with century-old brownstones. Franklin and Eleanor Roosevelt raised their burgeoning family in the town house at 2131 R from 1916 to 1920, when FDR was the dashing young assistant secretary of the Navy. The house is now the residence of the ambassador of Mali and cannot be visited. The flower-banked marble steps near the corner of 22nd and Decatur Street have been dubbed "The Spanish Steps," even though they bear not the slightest resemblance to the original staircase in Rome. Anyway, they are all that remains of Kalorama (Greek for "beautiful view"), the eighteenth-century manor house that gave this neighborhood its name.

A left turn on S Street leads past the Irish Embassy, with a harp over the entrance, to the *Textile Museum,* which just might be the best-kept secret in a city notorious for its leaks and indiscretions. The museum is the creation of George Hewitt Myers (as in Bristol-Myers), whose life-long love of the textile arts began with an Oriental rug in his dorm room at Yale. Seven decades later, Myers's undergraduate hobby has become a world-class collection of more than 14,000 textiles and 1,400 carpets that are housed in the elegant rooms of his former town home and the mansion next door. The museum's regular holdings include every conceivable example of the textile arts throughout the ages, from fifth-century Coptic and Islamic textiles and pre-Colombian textiles from Peru down to twentieth-century native weavings from Central America and New Mexico, all splendidly displayed under brilliant spotlights that accentuate their dazzling colors and intricate designs. The museum also hosts visiting collections, often with original themes, including the recent pairing of subtly patterned Amish quilts with boldly colored nineteenth-century Caucasian rugs.

And the gift shop is not to be missed. Just like the visual excitement of the museum's exhibits, its shop, located in the Myerses' former library, is one of the most colorful, attractive—and jumbled—you'll find anywhere; aside from reproductions of classic textiles in various forms, it

DUPONT CIRCLE

also offers a fine selection of books on the textile arts. The Textile Museum, 2320 S Street NW (667–0441, www.textilemuseum.org), is open Monday through Saturday 10:00 A.M. to 5:00 P.M., Sunday 1:00 to 5:00 P.M. Docent-led tours can be reserved two weeks in advance. Suggested admission contribution of $5.00.

These days, presidents usually hotfoot it out of town the minute their terms end, but in March 1921, when Woodrow Wilson left office, he actually stayed on in Washington, moving from 1600 Pennsylvania across town to an elegant Georgian Revival home that immediately became nationally known as "the house on S Street." Although the world Wilson helped create at Versailles has changed beyond recognition, his Washington town house has remained much as it was when he died there in 1924. Its combination of personal belongings and White House memorabilia makes **Woodrow Wilson House** both a fascinating presidential museum and a wonderfully preserved upper-class home of the 1920s, from the Wilsons' windup Victrola ready to play a 78 of "Oh You Beautiful Doll" to the box of Kellogg's "Pep" on the kitchen table. Wandering in this time warp, visitors find it easy to imagine that the Wilsons stepped out only a moment ago for a drive in nearby Rock Creek Park.

Wilson House docents say that for most visitors the real center of the house is Wilson's library, a comfortable and cluttered retreat filled with the personal and official mementos of his presidency. Wilson's cabinet chair is pushed back from a desk covered with personal papers; nearby stands a vintage microphone used for a 1923 broadcast. There's a "Graphoscope" movie projector (a 1913 gift from Douglas Fairbanks), and on the wall hangs a map of the brave but fleeting new Europe created by Wilson at Versailles. The house contains many personal and poignant touches. In the living room his massive Steinway and its period sheet music await the former president; in the upstairs bedroom, where Wilson died, a suit, walking stick, and boater are laid out for the next day's activities. A few steps away, in the nurse's room, we see a crude "shock stimulator" used in treating the paralyzed ex-president in his final months. Woodrow Wilson House, 2340 S Street NW (387–4062), is open Tuesday through Sunday 10:00 A.M. to 4:00 P.M. Admission is $5.00.

After leaving the Wilson House you'll be *(a)* standing at 24th and S Streets and *(b)* confronted with two choices, both of which represent

Florida Bound

*F*lorida Avenue, the western boundary of the Dupont Circle area was, in Colonial times, the main highway between the port of Georgetown and New York and New England; George Washington traveled it frequently. Known as Boundary Road in the nineteenth century, it was just that—the District's outer limit.

an embarrassment of riches for a wonderful stroll. Make that decision the Washington way and waffle. Take both and you'll be doing just like the local politicians, who often feel very strongly about something— both ways.

Your first option is to explore *Kalorama,* one of Washington's and the nation's finest residential neighborhoods. To do this, turn right and walk up 24th Street to explore side streets like California Street, Wyoming Avenue, and Tracy Place, which you'll find lined with elegant homes designed for America's super-rich by some of the foremost architects of their time. The forest of colorful flags along these streets tells you that most of these homes are now inhabited by foreign ambassadors. One of them is the Tudor mansion at 2221 Kalorama Road, built in 1911 for a mining millionaire, but is now, as you can see from the mammoth tricolor floating from the facade, the residence of the French ambassador.

Close by, at 2401 Kalorama Road, stands what I think is Washington's most magnificent house, *The Lindens,* a wonderful frame Georgian home with the look of Colonial New England. And well it should—The Lindens was actually built in Danvers, Massachusetts, in 1754, but in 1934 was dismantled and moved to Washington in sections. Check out the house's windows, which are originals, and the lovely little park and garden that surrounds it. Georgetown's Stone House is the oldest house *built* in Washington, but The Lindens is Washington's oldest house.

If the idea of living in this elegant neighborhood appeals to you, if only for a few nights, then check into the *Windsor Park Hotel,* a great budget find at 2116 Kalorama Road (corner of Connecticut Avenue); 483–7700, www.windsorparkhotel.com. This clean and comfortable boutique hotel, with its forty nicely furnished rooms, gets a big play from foreign diplomats in town to consult at their Washington embassies and from Americans lured by its optimal location for bus travel all over the city. Inexpensive.

Your other possibility is to return to Dupont Circle from 24th and S Streets, strolling past the most splendid palaces of Embassy Row. The opulence starts right away with the Embassy of Cameroon's imposing French château at 2349 Massachusetts, which is one of Washington's premiere Beaux Arts palaces. Architects know this romantic pile as the *Hauge House,* named for the wealthy Norwegian diplomat who built it in 1906. Speaking of Beaux Arts, wandering along Embassy Row you'll see a number of town houses similar to the Croatian Embassy—early twentieth-century buildings with French style that would feel right at home in Paris. The Croatian Embassy at 2343 Massachusetts also offers passersby a fine little statue by sculptor Ivan Mestrovic. Before reaching Sheridan Circle you also pass the magnificent Embassy of Haiti at 2311 and (ho-hum) yet another French château at 2315 that is now the Pakistani Embassy.

At Sheridan Circle, where General Phil Sheridan is spending his eternity directing traffic on horseback, look for the Mediterranean-style stucco house at 2306 Massachusetts. This was the home of Alice Pike Barney, who from 1902 to 1924 used the house as her studio and made it Washington's most dazzling artistic and literary salon. Lucky Washingtonians remember that until a few years ago Ms. Barney's flamboyant house and its paintings were open to the public. Not any more. The Smithsonian is now entrusted with the house, and plans for it are unclear.

On Sheridan Circle, between 23rd Street and Massachusetts Avenue, a small granite and bronze monument marks one of Washington's few successful acts of political terrorism. On this spot on September 21, 1976, a car bomb explosion killed former Chilean Ambassador Orlando Letelier and his American associate Roni Moffit. Chilean agents working for Gen. Agusto Pinochet were charged and convicted of this heinous crime.

Your walk to the Circle will take you past the Anderson House and then Washington's most overwhelming building, the *Walsh-McLean House* at 2020 Massachusetts. The house was built in 1903 by Thomas Walsh, a fabulously wealthy gold miner whose daughter, Evalyn Walsh McLean, went on to own the Hope diamond. Stupendous doesn't begin to describe this house, which boasts a grand stairwell copied from a *Titanic*-era ocean liner that Walsh took a shine to. The building is now the Embassy of Indonesia. Walk-in visits are not possible, but individual and group tours of the mansion can be requested by faxing the Embassy's Information Division at 775–5365 and stating your preferred dates and number of visitors.

Top-Secret Touring

*C*urious about what actually goes on inside those sumptuous embassies? If your CIA friend told you, he'd have to kill you, but there's an easier way to get that intelligence. In fact, two regular tours will let you crash those formidable gates.

The first is the **Goodwill Industries Embassy Tour,** which is held annually on the Saturday before Mother's Day from 10:00 A.M. to 5:00 P.M. Shuttle buses haul visitors all over Washington to see these distinguished dwellings. Tickets cost $30 if purchased in advance or $35 the day of the event.

For further information and to order tickets, call 636–4225, ext. 1226.

Another way is taking the **Kalorama House and Embassy Tour,** which takes place on the second Sunday in September from noon to 5:00 P.M. These self-guided walking tours start at the Wilson House, which sponsors this annual event, and visit both distinguished private homes and embassies throughout Kalorama. Tickets cost $18 when purchased in advance or $20 at the Wilson House on the day of the tour. For more details or to order tickets, call 387–4062, ext. 18.

One of the pleasures of wandering in this raffish area is poking into the lively shops and cafes that make the Circle a favorite of window shoppers and serious buyers. Dupont Circle is also ground zero for Washington's specialty book sellers, so bibliophiles, buyers, and browsers have a field day cruising the neighborhood. But don't forget to look up every now and then or you'll miss seeing that most of Connecticut Avenue's shops and cafes are lodged in what were once some of the city's grandest town houses.

Start your shopping at **Second Story Books,** at 20th and P Streets, a few steps from the Circle. Second Story gets its name from its first location as a small used book store over an Asian restaurant in northwest Washington. It is now one of the largest used and rare book stores in the world, with three outlets in the Washington area. The browsing is intense at Second Story, which is floor to ceiling, wall to wall books—a paradise for bibliophiles looking for rarities or anyone searching for that out-of-print book that was lent out but never seen again. In good weather the store sets up an outside remnants table with a well-earned reputation as a bargain-hunter's delight. Used CDs too. Second Story Books, 2000 P Street NW (659–8884, www.secondstorybooks.com), is open daily 10:00 A.M. to 10:00 P.M.

If you've been thinking that vinyl records are totally extinct, just stick your head into **Twelve Inches Dance Records,** for a look at one of the last outposts of the LP disk. This shop is always crowded with Washington-area DJs looking for new material for their clubs. We're not talking Vivaldi or Mantovani here, so the audition process can be a trifle noisy, as the jocks check out records by Onionz and Tony or Dilated Peoples on labels like Roc-a-Fella or, my favorite, Rawkus. Lots of fun, especially if you're into hip-hop. Twelve Inches Dance Records, on the second floor at 2010 P Street NW (659–2010), is open Monday through Thursday and Saturday noon to 9:00 P.M., Friday noon to 11:45 P.M., and Sunday 1:00 to 6:00 P.M.

Over on Connecticut Avenue you'll find the Circle's most concentrated shopping, beginning with **Kramerbooks,** one of Washington's top booksellers and one of a dwindling number of its independents. Kramerbooks' knowledgeable staff, personalized service, and impeccably selected inventory make this the perfect place to track down that special request or find the right book on everything from poetry to appreciating architecture to tips on souping up your sex life. Speaking of which, at the height of the Lewinsky scandal, Kramerbooks did all of us a favor by tearing up the Special Prosecutor's subpoena for its records of Monica's purchase of a book for President Clinton (since you asked, it was *Vox* by Nicholson Baker; if you read it you'll understand why it was a thoughtful gift). To read more about Kramer's principled (and costly) rejection of the Starr subpoena, check out the store's Web site at www.kramers.com.

Kramerbooks is also important if you're hungering for more than knowledge. Its **Afterwords Cafe and Grill** may be in the rear of the store, but it's a real restaurant and a good one, emphatically nothing like the little add-on cafes you'll find in many other bookstores.

Breakfasts are notable and inexpensive; the rest of the day you can order entree salads and sandwiches, while dinners can run the gamut from jumbo crab cakes to grilled fish and pastas. On Saturday and Sunday the Dupont literati gather here over brunch for profound, cholesterol-laden discussions of big topics. Kramerbooks and Afterwords Cafe, at 1517 Connecticut Avenue NW (387–1400), are both open Monday through Friday 7:30 A.M. to 1:00 A.M. and twenty-four hours on weekends.

In addition to being a social hub and information center for Dupont Circle's gay community, **Lambda Rising,** at 1625 Connecticut, is one of the most comprehensive gay/lesbian bookstores in the country. In fact, it was the original shop for what is now a national chain of bookstores for gay men and women. Lambda Rising (462–6969), is open Friday and Saturday 10:00 A.M. to midnight; the rest of the week it's 10:00 A.M. to 10:00 P.M.

GrapeFinds is probably the most dramatic wine store in the country. No jumble of dusty bottles, hastily scrawled price tags, or underlit shelves here, just a starkly attractive and beautifully illuminated display of top wines. Furthermore, co-owner (and professional wine consultant) Michael Green has arranged his wines unconventionally, by taste categories such as "fruity," "crisp," and "bold," making it easier for you to match wine with food. GrapeFinds, 1643 Connecticut Avenue (387–3146, www.grapefinds.com), is open Monday through Thursday 9:00 A.M. to 9:00 P.M., Friday until 10:00 P.M., Saturday until 11:00 P.M.

Don't get excited, *Xando* is not Hearst's castle, nor is it a pill that will take you to nirvana. Although Dupont Circle is a famously laid-back area, few coffeehouses manage to be as hip and mellow as this European-style cafe at 1647 20th Street at the corner of Connecticut. Xando offers coffee in every conceivable shape and form, along with a food menu that includes teas, sandwiches, and, for the nostalgic, s'mores (you toast the marshmallows). After 4:00 P.M. you can start adding booze to your order. Even the Web site, www.xando.com, is terminally cool. Call 332–6364. Open Monday through Thursday 6:30 A.M. to midnight, Friday 6:30 A.M. to 2:00 A.M., Saturday 7:00 A.M. to 2:00 A.M., and Sunday 7:00 A.M. to midnight.

Upon entering *Secondi,* it's hard to believe that you're in a consignment clothing store and not a trendy, definitely upscale boutique. There are serious bargains here, from recycled dinner gowns to barely worn designer dresses with labels that even some men will recognize. Alas, there's a touch of sexism here: All of this secondhand chic is only for women; no men's clothing sold. Secondi, upstairs at 1702 Connecticut Avenue, is open Monday, Tuesday, and Saturday 11:00 A.M. to 6:00 P.M., Wednesday through Friday 11:00 A.M. to 7:00 P.M., and Sunday 1:00 to 5:00 P.M. Call 667–1122.

To dine in an equally chic restaurant, walk across Connecticut Avenue to *La Tomate.* With its stark white walls, splashy paintings, and sunny

Down on the Dupont Farm

*I*t's a bit incongruous, but this highly sophisticated and hip neighborhood, better known for art than asparagus, has its own farmer's market. Every Sunday from 9:00 A.M. to 1:00 P.M. vendors congregate behind the Riggs Bank just off the Circle at the corner of Massachusetts and 20th Street to sell organic vegetables trucked in from neighboring states. You'll also find a good selection of flowers, exotic fruits, and even handwoven sweaters from Ecuador.

Capital Quote

"Washington was the one city in the east where any woman with money and talent could set up house-keeping and become an important hostess."

—*Alice Hoge, writing in*
Cissy Patterson

Mediterranean look, La Tomate might just have floated in from southern Europe. Those impressions are soon confirmed by a menu that is strong on pastas based on shellfish and vegetables, and second courses like spezzatino di pollo and veal Milanese. As a bonus, this "Italian bistro" has large sidewalk windows perfect for the people-watching that comes with the Dupont Circle territory. La Tomate, 1701 Connecticut Avenue, is open Monday through Thursday 11:30 A.M. to 10:30 P.M., Friday and Saturday 11:00 A.M. to 11:00 P.M., and Sunday 11:30 A.M. to 10:00 P.M. It's a good idea to reserve by calling 667–5505.

Mystery Books is another one of those specialized bookshops that makes exploring Dupont Circle so rewarding. This one's for mystery addicts; the shelves here are crammed with mystery and detective novels of all kinds, and there are 15,000 of them. Owner Tina McGill has thoughtfully spotted some cushy easy chairs among the shelves to make browsing comfortable. Add a coal fire and you'd swear you're upstairs at 221B Baker Street. In addition to its nationally recognized collection of titles, Mystery Books also hosts a number of signings by distinguished writers like P. D. James and Jeffrey Deaver. Mystery Books, 1715 Connecticut Avenue NW (483–1600, www.killerbooks.com), is open Monday through Friday 11:00 A.M. to 7:00 P.M., Saturday 10:00 A.M. to 6:00 P.M., Sunday noon to 5:00 P.M.

Ginza specializes in things Japanese, so you'll find a nice selection of Asian items there for your home, office, and garden, including samurai dolls, tea sets, lacquered boxes, and many books on Japan and its art. And if you really must have a samurai T-shirt, this is the place to get it. Ginza, 1721 Connecticut Avenue NW (331–7991), is open Monday through Saturday 11:00 A.M. to 7:00 P.M., Sunday noon to 6:00 P.M.

Another top neighborhood bookstore is *Kulturas Books,* which lives up to its name with a large selection of used books, many on politics, literary biography, and history. Poking around in this slightly frayed old-shoe shop can yield great finds, including the occasional rarity. Kulturas Books, 1741 Connecticut Avenue NW (462–2541), is open Monday through Wednesday 11:00 A.M. to 9:00 P.M., Thursday through Saturday 11:00 A.M. to 10:00 P.M., and Sunday 11:00 A.M. to 7:00 P.M.

If you're from out of town or another country and can't wait to find out what's going on back home, head for *The Newsroom,* which carries magazines and newspapers from practically everywhere. There's also a

Diplomatic Niceties

To avoid making a diplomatic gaffe that would embarrass your country, you should know that an embassy is where the ambassador lives. The building where he and his exalted flunkies have their offices is called the chancery.

large selection of language teaching manuals and materials. The Newsroom, at 1803 Connecticut Avenue (332–1489), is open 7:00 A.M. to 9:00 P.M. every day.

If you've had your fill of shopping, another good walk involves exploring the Dupont Circle neighborhood east of Connecticut Avenue beginning at 18th and Church Streets, where there's a lovely little garden rimmed with daffodils and azaleas that's just perfect for resting or picnicking. This was the site of *St. Thomas Episcopal Church,* a miniature Gothic cathedral where Franklin and Eleanor Roosevelt frequently worshipped. St. Thomas was destroyed by arson in 1970; all that remains of one of Washington's loveliest and most cherished churches is the fire-scorched north altar wall. Although St. Thomas may physically be gone, its sense of tranquillity lingers on in the park, and its parishioners still hold services in the adjoining rectory, which was undamaged by the fire.

Even die-hard Republicans like to take a bipartisan peek at the *Women's National Democratic Club,* which is located in the delightful Whittemore House, an 1892 charmer built in a free-form, slightly undulating shape with protruding dormer windows and a gorgeous caped roof. Beyond the house's wood paneled entrance hall, a series of spacious and handsomely furnished rooms commemorates Democratic First Ladies—especially Eleanor Roosevelt, a frequent visitor—and leaders of the suffrage movement. The Women's National Democratic Club, 1526 New Hampshire Avenue NW (232–7363), is open Monday through Saturday 10:00 A.M. to 5:00 P.M.

Farther up 18th Street, at the corner of New Hampshire Avenue, you'll see the Beaux Arts prow of one of Washington's most spectacular homes, the fifty-four-room *Belmont Mansion,* which could have floated in from Versailles. The house now belongs to the Order of the Eastern Star, which, because of the ultrasecret paraphernalia within, admits only members of the Order or of Masonic orders (application at the door). If you get in, you'll pass through a regal entrance hall, then a granite double staircase and go upstairs where, I'm told, the state dining room sports a ceiling from the doge's palace in Venice. If you're not cleared, you'll have to settle for standing outside and admiring the magnificent Louis XIV style of the building and its lovely gardens of unclassified tulips and azaleas.

Around the corner on R Street, the **National Museum of American Jewish Military History,** which operates under the auspices of the Jewish War Veterans of the U.S.A., documents the contributions that Jewish men and women have made to American military efforts in every war. The museum's exhibits include medals, weapons, and other military memorabilia, along with photos, diaries, and letters from the museum's large photographic and documentary archive. Recent shows have included the story of General Julius Klein's service as a teenage spy in World War I and a major general in World War II, as well as profiles of Jewish women in the military and Jews who fought in the Civil War and the Revolution. The museum, at 1811 R Street NW (265–6280, www. penfed.org/jwv/museum.htm), is open Monday through Friday 9:00 A.M. to 5:00 P.M. and Sunday 1:00 to 5:00 P.M.; closed Saturdays and Jewish holidays. Contributions appreciated. E-mail: jwv@erols.com.

Now you're nearing the point on 18th Street where Dupont Circle ends and the area known as **Adams Morgan** begins. Adams Morgan (or Madam's Organ, as it is sometimes called) is one of the District's most tumultuous neighborhoods and a social center of the city's Latino, Caribbean, and African residents. Perfectly routine and quiet by day, Adams Morgan really comes to life at night, when it becomes Washington's liveliest restaurant scene. If you go, keep in mind that Adams Morgan has no Metro station, that the Dupont Circle stop is at least thirty minutes away, and that the parking situation is catastrophic. Take a cab. Here are a few restaurants to think about:

I Matti, 2436 18th Street (462–8844), is one of the top trattorias in town. A casual and lively place with terrific pastas, including sea food *al cartoccio,* game (try the rabbit cutlet with prosciutto and cheese), and great pizzas, especially the Margherita. If you've been yearning for osso

Museum Meander

*N*ine leading museums and arts sites welcome visitors and provide special musical and other programs during the annual **Dupont-Kalorama Museum Walk,** held on the first weekend of June. The Phillips Collection sponsors hands-on art activities for children, the Fondo del Sol Visual Arts Center goes aural with live Latin music, and there's sheepshearing at the Textile Museum. A free shuttle will take you around, stopping at each site on Saturday from 10:00 A.M. to 4:00 P.M., and Sunday 1:00 to 5:00 P.M. Call 667–0441 for full information.

buco ever since your stay in Milan, I Matti is definitely for you. What else? Well, there's a calorie-packed dessert cart and a well-priced wine list. Reservations are essential. Moderate.

In spite of the pun, the **Grill from Ipanema** is a top Brazilian restaurant, where you can guzzle caipirinhas, made with limes, sugar, and million-proof rum. It's a good idea to have only one before ordering conch chowder, Brazilian grilled meat, or Brazil's national dish, feijoada, a feast of black beans, brined beef, sausage, and cuts of pork. The restaurant is at 1858 Columbia Road NW; 986–0757. Inexpensive.

Cashion's Eat Place, 1819 Columbia Road NW (797–1819), will remind you of a 1937 Parisian bistro—the intimate atmosphere, the bar with habitués sitting under a painting of a nude, and more than a whiff of romance in the air; somewhere cool jazz is playing. The food is even better than the setting, an eclectic menu that swings from roast leg of lamb, duck breast with foie gras, or veal cheeks. Chef-owner Ann Cashion changes the menu daily, but not to worry, you'll be in good hands. Reservations are a must, especially for the yummy Sunday brunch. Moderate.

A good way to sample the Adams Morgan ethnic mix is a meal at **Rocky's Cafe,** which serves up dishes with the flavors and aromas of Africa, the Caribbean, and the American south. This is the place to order up a platter of jerk chicken wings, some sweet potato fries or red beans and rice. Great atmosphere with eclectic music. Rocky's is at 1817 Columbia Road NW; 387–2580. Inexpensive.

PLACES TO STAY IN DUPONT CIRCLE

The Carlyle Suites, 1731 New Hampshire Avenue NW; 234–3200 or (800) 964–5377, fax 387–0085. This converted apartment house on one of Dupont Circle's quieter residential streets announces its art deco origins in a lobby covered with louvered sconces and other Chrysler Build-ing touches. The Carlyle, with its 170 comfortable suites with mini kitchens and dining areas, offers comfort and value, especially for families. The handsome restaurant, open daily 6:30 A.M. to 2:00 P.M. and 5:00 to 10:00 P.M., offers mainly light fare such as pastas, soup, and sandwiches, but also grills steaks and fish. Moderate.

Swann House, 1808 New Hampshire Avenue NW; 265–4414, www.swann house.com. This is one of the District's few B&Bs, and it's a good one. This redbrick Victorian mansion, which was built in 1883 by a noted Washington architect and artist, has more than its share of elegant period touches—the crown moldings, 12-foot ceilings, inlaid floors, and other features you'd expect from a Victorian beauty. But more to the point, many of its twelve spacious rooms come with tasteful antiques, working fireplaces, and whopping bathrooms, plus fax machines and dataport phones that make Swann House a business favorite. And, thankfully, not an antimacassar or sherry bottle anywhere in sight. Swann House also has its own swimming pool, which is small, but just what you want during those sizzling Washington summers. Moderate.

The Canterbury, 1733 N Street NW; 393–3000, fax 785–9581. In a neighborhood that's a little short on hotel possibilities, it's worth knowing about The Canterbury, an all-suite hotel with European touches. Each suite has a modern galley kitchen, a dressing room, and closets large enough for an archbishop. A great location for sightseeing will make it easy for you to start collecting your own Canterbury Tales. Moderate.

Hotel Tabard Inn, 1739 N Street NW; 785–1277, fax 785–6173. A British writer once described this inn as "the sort of place favored by Englishmen who prefer 'character' to room service and by Americans who want to assert their individuality." That's a pretty good description of this

Where to Find The Author's Favorite Places to Stay in Dupont Circle

Windsor Park Hotel
2116 Kalorama Road; 483–7700
(see page 130 for full listing)

small, laid-back hotel with a distinctly British feel: big rooms with Victorian decor, occasionally quirky furnishings, and moderate prices. Also notable is the hotel's restaurant, a cozy, casual favorite with the locals. Moderate.

Jury's Doyle Washington, 1500 New Hampshire Avenue NW; 483–6000. Because it's right on the Circle and next to the Metro station, you can't get much more centrally located than this D.C. outpost of Ireland's largest hotel group. The hotel's 300 plus attractive rooms are often filled with business travelers and foreign officials visiting on State Department grants, so it pays to reserve in advance. The Irish theme carries over into the hotel's atmospheric pub, where Bushmill's is the national pastime, and its restaurant, where, you'll be happy to hear, the cooking is better than in Dublin. Moderate.

PLACES TO EAT IN DUPONT CIRCLE

Rosemary's Thyme, 1801 18th Street NW; 332–3200. The food at Rosemary's Thyme is as handsome and lively as the surroundings in this "Mediterranean-Creole bistro," which is saying a lot. You come here for big salads, shellfish pastas, unbelievable lamb shanks, and a long list of kabobs; wraps of freshly baked *pide,* a Turkish flat bread, are another specialty. The long and fairly priced wine list is a plus. Reservations recommended. Open Monday through Friday 11:30 A.M. to 11:00 P.M., Saturday 11:00 A.M. to midnight, and Sunday 11:00 A.M. to 11:00 P.M. Moderate.

Beduci, 2100 P Street NW; 223–3824. You'll find a mix of Mediterranean cooking here, with the accent on Spain, Italy, and France. The restaurant's name, however, is strictly homegrown, meaning "below

Dupont Circle." Main courses include pastas with shellfish and sautéed or grilled fish, game chops, a few exotic meats such as grilled ostrich, plus the predictable paella and couscous. The wine list is long, Mediterranean oriented, and, except for some Sicilian bargains, a bit pricey. Open Monday through Friday 11:30 A.M. to 10:30 P.M., Friday and Saturday 5:15 P.M. to 10:30 P.M., Sunday 5:30 to 9:30 P.M. Expensive.

Johnny's Half Shell, 2002 P Street NW; 296–2021. Johnny's is a great restaurant find for anyone seeking sustenance in the Dupont Circle area. Fish is the speciality at this small, cheery restaurant just off the Circle. Johnny's dense, peppery seafood gumbo is almost a meal in itself, but why stop there when you can move on to the terrific crab cakes, a *fritto misto* of fried shrimp, calamari, and monkfish, or arguably the best fish and chips in town? A short but well-conceived wine list rounds out the pleasure. No reservations taken, but the wait, which can be considerable, is worth it. Open Monday through Friday 11:30 A.M. to 10:30 P.M., Saturday 11:30 A.M. to 11:30 P.M.; closed Sunday. Moderate.

Where to Find the Author's Favorite Places to Eat in Dupont Circle

Brickskeller
1523 22nd Street NW; 293–1885
(see page 125 for full listing)

Afterwords Cafe and Grill
1517 Connecticut Avenue NW; 387–1400
(see page 133 for full listing)

Xando
1647 20th Street; 332–6364
(see page 134 for full listing)

La Tomate
1701 Connecticut Avenue; 667–5505
(see page 134 for full listing)

I Matti
2436 18th Street; 462–8844
(see page 137 for full listing)

Grill from Ipanema
858 Columbia Road NW; 986–0757
(see page 138 for full listing)

Cashion's Eat Place
1819 Columbia Road NW; 797–1819
(see page 138 for full listing)

Rocky's Cafe
1817 Columbia Road NW; 387–2580
(see page 138 for full listing)

Midi, 1635 Connecticut Avenue NW; 234–3090. This attractive self-service restaurant with a French country feel dishes up great French toast (of course) and other breakfast favorites, while lunches include vegan salads, pizzette, and sandwiches. At dinner the Midi's rotisserie churns out moist herbed chicken and vegetarian lasagna. Open Monday through Saturday 8:00 A.M. to 9:30 P.M., Sunday 8:00 A.M. to 8:00 P.M. Inexpensive.

The Obelisk, 2029 P Street; 872–1180. Located in a town house, this might be the city's best Italian restaurant. The Obelisk has a short but exquisite fixed price menu (at this writing $55), and it varies nightly. On our latest visit the antipasti choices included peppers prepared with vegetables and cheese or stuffed pig's foot. The first course involved deciding between halibut raviolini and gnocchi with Gorgonzola cheese, while the entree possibilities included veal tenderloin with juniper relish, pan-cooked grouper, and roast squab with mushrooms and polenta. Memorable desserts and wines too. Reservations are essential. Open Tuesday through Saturday 6:00 to 10:00 P.M. Expensive.

Shaw and U Street

As soon as you see the stunning mural of Duke Ellington on the wall opposite the Lincoln Theater, you have a pretty good idea of what this neighborhood is all about. Music in general and the Duke in particular are the soul of Shaw, an area that for decades has been Washington's answer to New York's Harlem and Chicago's Bronzeville. Shaw is the traditional center of the city's black cultural, professional, and educational world in what was for many years a strictly segregated national capital. An intellectual hub as well, Shaw is the home of Howard University, founded during Reconstruction in 1867, a magnet for American black leaders and still one of our premier historically black universities.

Unique among Washington's neighborhoods, Shaw has always been black, starting in Civil War days when freed slaves began living modestly in what was then a rural setting within the District. Black professionals erected their own homes in Shaw during Reconstruction, and began to form a cultural and social legacy that made Washington the center of African-American life in the United States. One result has been that this area has some of the city's handsomest Victorian row houses and business buildings, mostly built, financed, and designed by African-Americans.

Duke Ellington grew up in Shaw, at 1212 T Street in the years before World War I, when U Street was a musical mecca. During those years the clubs along U Street, Washington's elegant "Black Broadway," made the neighborhood the center of African-American cabaret and social life, especially in the 1920s and 1930s, when ragtime and cakewalk began to morph into "jass." Duke played his first gig ever on the top floor of the True Reformer's Hall at 12th and U, a building now being renovated, after which he advertised in the Washington Yellow Pages that he and his band of "colored syncopaters" were open for business.

Already in decline since the 1950s, U Street was hard hit by the 1968 riots that followed Martin Luther King Jr.'s assassination, after which the area became an urban war zone, where drug markets, crack houses, and vice of every kind flourished. Happily, Shaw is now in the midst of

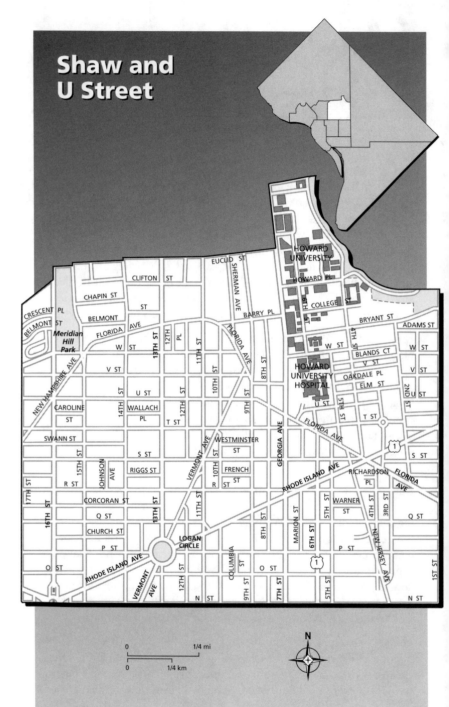

Shaw and U Street

SHAW AND U STREET

Top Attractions in
Shaw and U Street

Lincoln Theater

The Whitelaw

*Mary McLeod Bethune
Council House*

Logan Circle

*African-American Civil
War Memorial*

Ben's Chili Bowl

a vigorous recovery. Historic buildings are being restored and the neighborhood is experiencing a minor real estate boom, with new dwellings being built and historic ones being renovated by black upscale professionals, known hereabouts as "buppies." And on 14th Street, once Washington's "automobile row," plays and concerts are drawing theatergoers to a street that is slowly recovering from the trauma of 1968.

Best of all, nightlife is once again flourishing along U Street. The *Washington Post* attributes its recovery to the coming of the Metro in 1991 and a gentrification movement that has affected much of the District. Whatever the reason, U Street is back and, although you'll still want to exercise the usual nighttime caution, it's once again an area where Washingtonians go to enjoy nightlife and have a good time.

Another local community now undergoing revitalization is **Le Droit Park,** an urban enclave with a definite small-town feel and quiet streets with names like Spruce, Elm, and Larch. Its architecture is also small town, mostly 1870 vintage romantic Victorian, with styles like Queen Anne and Gothic cottage. Le Droit Park has traditionally been associated with the intellectual life of its neighbor, Howard University, and has been the home of many black leaders and educators, including the Reverend Jesse Jackson and the Duke himself, who lived at 420 Elm Street NW.

But we'll start our tour a few blocks away at **Logan Circle,** the epicenter of some of Washington's most elegant architecture, a treasure trove of grand Victorian town houses and mansions. Logan Circle's ongoing restoration and historic preservation present a classic example of how a neighborhood can be restored and revived through community cooperation.

After taking in the grand homes that ring the Circle, head down Vermont Avenue to the **Mary McLeod Bethune Council House.** At this handsome Victorian town house just off Logan Circle, you'll find the museum and archives that preserve and interpret the life of one of the great figures in African-American history, the remarkable woman who became a friend and valued adviser on minority matters to Eleanor and Franklin Roosevelt. Before coming to Washington to advise the Roosevelts, Bethune was already a prominent political activist for black causes and an educator who founded the school that is today Florida's Bethune-Cookman College.

The ground level parlor holds mementos of Ms. Bethune, including her grand piano and photographs of her and her colleagues in the black women's movement. In the rear a video traces the history of the movement and the close relationship Ms. Bethune established with both Roosevelts. On the same level you'll see an excellent bookstore and shop with items dedicated to African-American history. Upstairs, in Bethune's bedroom, more pictures and photographs capture the essence of a remarkable life. The house also holds extensive archives of the National Council of Negro Women, which she founded in 1935, and other documents connected with the struggle of African-American women. The Mary McLeod Bethune Council House, 1318 Vermont Avenue NW (673–2402, www.nps.gov/mamc), is open Monday through Saturday 10:00 A.M. to 4:00 P.M. Access to the archives is by appointment only; to get one, call the archivist at 673–2402. Metro: McPherson Square (orange and blue lines).

The **Studio Theater,** at 1338 P Street NW, offers three stages of performances of contemporary theater. In its twenty-three years, the studio has earned a national reputation and praise in the national press for innovative, imaginative theater and, along the way, has garnered dozens of national awards. To find what's playing during your visit, call the box office at 332–3300, or drop in between 10:00 A.M. and 6:00 P.M., Monday through Friday. For a virtual visit, it's www.studiotheatre.org. Metro: U Street–Cardozo (green line).

At 1401 Church Street NW, just off 14th Street, you'll find the **Woolly Mammoth,** what the *New York Times* called "Washington's most daring theater company." Woolly mammoths may be slightly antiquated, but that's the last thing you'd say about this cutting-edge theater, which puts on shows with titles like *Preaching to the Perverted* and other edgy American plays. The Woolly is now in its twentieth season and is still going strong. If you're interested in seeing some of Washington's most original and talented theater, call 393–3939 for details or go to www.woolly mammoth.net on the Web. Metro: U Street–Cardozo (green line).

Diversite, located in a former car salesroom along what was once Washington's "automobile row" is now part Italian restaurant and part Latino music mecca. The plan is simple: dinner featuring Italian specialties followed by live Latin music. There's also a great selection of CDs, so you can't go wrong. And since this was once a showroom and repair area, there's plenty of room for dancing, and you'll have lots of company. Diversite, 1526 14th Street NW (234–5740), is open Sunday through Thursday 4:00 to 11:00 P.M., Friday and Saturday 4:00 P.M. to 3:30 A.M. Moderate. Metro: U Street–Cardozo (green line).

SHAW AND U STREET

AUTHOR'S FAVORITES IN SHAW AND U STREET

African-American Civil War Memorial

Lincoln Theater

Logan Circle

Ben's Chili Bowl

U-topia

Florida Avenue Grill

Jazz aficionados will definitely want to think about visiting *HR57,* where open mike, straight-ahead jazz sessions lure crowds every Wednesday and Friday night. The sessions here are laid-back and impromptu, and usually feature visiting or local professional musicians. HR57, more formally known as the Center for the Preservation of Jazz and Blues, takes its name from the 1987 House Resolution that designated jazz as an American treasure. And you'll hear the best of it here in this storefront jazz mecca. There's also a set dinner each night, usually fried chicken, red beans and rice, and potato salad, not to mention the ambrosial fresh lemonade. The action at HR57, 1610 14th Street NW (667–3700), starts at 8:30 P.M. on Wednesday and 9:00 P.M. on Friday. Admission is $6.00; the fixed-price dinner will run you another $6.00. Metro: U Street–Cardozo (green line).

At 14th and U, you've reached the epicenter of this historic neighborhood. A left turn leads to *U-topia,* one of the area's most popular and laid-back restaurants. Here you'll find a good selection of bar food and light fare with a Cajun touch, including dishes like spicy gumbos and chicken jambalaya. U-topia's Sunday brunch from 11:00 A.M. to 4:00 P.M. is, to say the least, abundant, provided you make it through the potent $1.00 mimosas and Bloody Marys. No reservations. Dining hours: Monday through Friday 6:00 P.M. to midnight; Saturday and Sunday 10:00 A.M. to midnight. U-topia also offers very significant jazz action on Thursday from 9:30 P.M. to 1:00 A.M., Friday and Saturday 10:30 P.M. to 2:30 A.M., and Sunday 9:30 P.M. to 1:30 A.M. Inexpensive. Metro: U Street–Cardozo (green line).

A right turn takes you down U Street past *Polly's,* at 1342 U Street NW (265–8385). This neighborhood favorite is cool and laid-back, with great music to listen to by the fire. The excellent bar food is another reason Polly pulls them in, with a menu that offers top-notch burgers, portobello mushroom steaks, and fried calamari. Open Monday through Friday 6:00 P.M. to 2:00 A.M., Saturday and Sunday 10:00 A.M. to 2:00 A.M. Inexpensive to moderate.

If you're taking this stroll on Saturday or Sunday between 7:00 A.M. and 5:00 P.M., you'll find a thriving flea market in full swing on U Street in the parking lot between 13th and 14th Streets. Drop by to find books, furniture, posters, and the latest in legible clothing.

The Whitelaw, at 1839 13th Street NW, is now a sparkling 1919 Beaux Arts apartment house offering affordable housing to local residents.

The Howard Theater

One Shaw musical land-mark yet to be restored and saved from decay is the Howard Theater, a sump-tuous palace at Seventh and T Streets NW, which opened in 1910. This is where Ellington and other jazz greats like Jelly Roll Morton and Ella Fitzgerald performed regularly. Unfortunately, it is unre-stored and falling into decay and is emphatically not open to visitors.

But until 1945 it was the only hotel in Washington open to blacks. Duke Ellington stayed there, as did Cab Calloway, Joe Louis, and many other visiting notables. During its depths in the '50s and '60s the Whitelaw was a notorious drug den and bordello that was finally closed because of its dilapidated condition, not to mention its rep-utation. Thanks to a combination of local fund-ing and community pride, the Whitelaw has been beautifully restored to its former elegance. Especially striking is the graceful dining room, with its original stained glass ceiling. Because people live there, you can't just wander around, but if you ring the bell marked *office* and ask nicely, you just might get in. It's worth it.

No doubt about it, the **Lincoln Theater** is one of Washington's hidden treasures. When it was built in 1922, the Lincoln was where African-Americans could watch vaudeville shows and first-run films in a city whose theaters were strictly segregated. Duke Ellington and Count Basie also played there, in a mammoth ballroom that once stood behind the current theater. The Lincoln was for years the heart and soul of black cul-tural and social life, but during the 1950s it fell on hard times. Restored to its original glory in 1994, today it's one of Washington's great interior spaces, where you walk off a busy street into the gilt, architectural detail, and plush of an elegant theater of the 1920s. Call the box office at 328–6000 for details of the Lincoln's rich cultural programs, which include plays, concerts, and dance and film festivals. The Lincoln Theater, 1215 U Street NW, is across the street from the 13th Street exit of the U Street–Cardozo Metro station on the green line and the Duke's portrait.

If there were a Michelin guide to Washington, you'd find **Ben's Chili Bowl,** at 1231 U, marked with the red symbols that mean "restaurant of habitues," i.e., all the smart locals hang out there because it's so great. Ben's building was once the Minnehaha Theater, in its day one of the best, which advertised "clean vaudeville" acts. But since 1958 Ben's has been a gathering place for everyone in black Washington, from night workers to students at nearby Howard University to Bill Cosby, who's been coming here for years for the chili half smokes. And you might, as I did, spot Michael Jordan folded into one of Ben's booths. Ben's atmosphere probably resembles those places you knew in the '50s—formica lunch counters with stools, shiny red plastic chairs, and food served right from the grill. Ben's dishes will also take you back to all those precholesterol days, with dishes like half smokes or Kosher hot dogs doused with spicy chili, not to mention breakfasts highlighted by eggs and scrapple or sausages, or hot cakes with grits or home fries. Funky music too. It's wonderful! Be still my heart (note to my cardiologist: just kidding!). Ben's Chili Bowl, 1213 U Street NW (667–0909), is open Monday through Thursday 6:00 A.M. to 2:00 A.M., Saturday 7:00 A.M. to 4:00 A.M., Sunday noon to 8:00 P.M. Reservations—are you kidding? Inexpensive. Metro: Shaw–Howard U (green line).

One of the great finds during the preparation of this guide was *The Islander,* a modest storefront at 1201 U Street specializing in Caribbean cookery, with a friendly atmosphere just as relaxed as the islands themselves. The dishes show the islands' African/East Indian roots. Start off with callaloo (a spinach-okra mix) or plantain, then shift into high gear with the excellent calypso chicken with a mild red sauce, roti, a curried wrap with Indian overtones, or a curried shrimp or goat accompanied by peleau (fried chickpeas and rice) and a bottle of Trinidadian beer. The Islander is open Tuesday through Thursday noon to 11:00 P.M., until 1:00 A.M. Friday and Saturday, and Sunday 1:00 to 6:00 P.M. Live jazz most Sundays from 7:00 to 11:00 P.M. Metro: Shaw–Howard U (green line). Call 234–4955.

At the intersection of U Street and Vermont Avenue, the *African-American Civil War Memorial,* one of Washington's newest national memorials, honors the 210,000 black troops who fought with the "U.S. Colored Troops" during the Civil War. The names of those soldiers are inscribed on this open-air memorial's polished metal tablets and are guarded by

Tell 'em "Off the Beaten Path" Sent You

*G*oing to **Signal 66** *is like visiting a 1920s speakeasy—walk down an alley to a nondescript door marked "926 N," where a buzzer will admit you to a former livery stable that is now one of the District's most exciting arts and communications spaces. Entering the high-ceilinged exhibit space, you might find a "warehouse party" in progress, along with shows by local and other artists in the gallery's three studios. Signal 66 is also the home of a recording studio and Web site operated by its three artist-owners. Signal 66, at the rear of 926 N Street NW, is open Thursday noon to 5:00 P.M., Friday 5:00 to 8:00 P.M., and Saturday noon to 6:00 P.M. Find out what's going on by calling 842–3436 or going to www.signal66. com. The issue-oriented Web site operated at the gallery is www.planetvox.com. Metro: Mt. Vernon Square–UDC (yellow line).*

African-American Civil War Memorial

a statue, *Spirit of Freedom,* depicting a group of African-Americans who fought in the Union Army. The names of the soldiers are listed by regiment, one of which is the famous 53rd Massachusetts, which fought with distinction at the battles of Forts Pillow and Wagner under a white colonel, Robert Shaw (for whom this area is named); their bravery was dramatized in the film *Glory.* The memorial is located at the entrance to the U Street–Cardozo Metro at Tenth and U Streets NW, but its impressive Information Center and Museum is at 1000 U, just around the corner. The center is open Monday through Friday 9:00 A.M. to 5:00 P.M., weekends 2:00 to 5:00 P.M. Call 667–2667.

The **Black Fashion Museum** is dedicated to the contributions that African-Americans have made to fashion and design. This century-old row house highlights Elizabeth Keckley, a former slave who designed Mary Lincoln's dresses and was also her personal confidante; a copy of a Keckley design for Mrs. Lincoln is a major attraction. Another important exhibit honors an already famous Ann Lowe, who in 1953 designed Jackie Kennedy's wedding gown. The Black Fashion Museum, 2007 Vermont Avenue NW, is open only by appointment. To get one, call 667–0744 or e-mail bfmdc@aol.com. Internet: www.bfmdc.org. Metro: U Street–Cardozo (green line).

To the northwest lies the Meridian Hill Section of the city. The area gets its name from the zero meridian of the United States, which Thomas Jefferson placed along 16th Street; a boundary stone once stood at the corner of Florida and 16th. In the nineteenth century its high ground and panoramic views made Meridian Hill an enclave of the wealthy and helped turn 16th Street into the city's earlier Embassy Row. A number of Embassies remain there, but many more have left because of security concerns. Meridian Hill's decline, however, seems to have halted; in recent years, the area has begun to revive and recover. Since there is no handy Metro stop, think car or taxi.

Two of the neighborhood's great homes remain and attract visitors; both are owned by the Meridian International Center, a nonprofit educational and cultural institution that seeks to promote international understanding through exchanges of people, ideas, and the arts. The center also sponsors a wide-ranging schedule of briefings, lectures, and other programs on global issues.

The thirty-room *Meridian House,* at 1630 Crescent Place NW, was built in 1920 by steel heir and career diplomat Irwin Laughlin, as in Jones and Laughlin. Shortly after it was completed, the House was called "one of the finest examples of architecture in the French style in America." Sorry to say, Meridian House is open to the public only for weddings, receptions, and other social events. However, you don't have to get married to wander through the house's lovely terraced garden or peer through the French doors into a vanished world and the public rooms of a classic European château.

Meridian House's next-door neighbor, the *White-Meyer House* (667–6800, www.meridian.org), was built in 1911 for Henry White, a former ambassador to France, but was occupied from 1929 until 1971 by Eugene Meyer, the publisher of the *Washington Post.* The grand rooms of the White-Meyer House now host a series of internationally oriented art and cultural exhibits on a rotating basis; check the *Post's Weekend* magazine for the latest schedule. The White-Meyer House, at 1624 Crescent Place NW, is usually open Tuesday through Sunday 2:00 to 5:00 P.M.; because there are a number of special events, it's a good idea to call ahead.

Meridian Hill Park, at 16th and W Streets across from the two mansions, is both part of the National Park system and a neighborhood park that will remind you of Rome's Borghese Gardens or Villa Medici. Because of its terraces and dramatic water cascade with thirteen pools, experts call this Renaissance villa park a masterpiece of landscape architecture. It's also an agreeable place where local families take their kids during the day, but avoid after sunset. So should you.

PLACES TO STAY IN SHAW AND U STREET

Shipman House Bed and Breakfast, 1310 Q Street NW; 328–3510, www.bbonline.com/dc/the reeds/index. This 1887 Victorian home has been nicely converted by innkeepers Charles and Jackie Reed into a B&B that has received national press attention for its restoration and elegant features. The House abounds in period touches like stained glass windows and grand fireplaces, not to mention its luxurious paneled rooms and garden with fountains. The Shipman House has six guest rooms that will take you straight back to those never-to-be-forgotten days of Grover Cleveland and Rutherford B. Hayes. For longer stays the Reeds also offer a self-contained apartment. Inexpensive. Metro: Shaw/Howard University (green line).

PLACES TO EAT IN SHAW AND U STREET

Mar de Plata, 1410 14th Street NW; 234–2679. Hot and cold tapas like seafood salad, grilled sausage, and fried pork with cassava are the specialties in this bright and cheerful Spanish storefront. You can make a meal of the tapas or forge ahead to second courses like paella, *carne guisada* (Spanish for a tasty beef stew), and grilled salmon. A good selection of Spanish wines and sherries plus service that makes you feel that *estas en tu casa.* Open Tuesday through Sunday noon to 3:00 P.M. and 4:00 P.M. to midnight, and Monday 4:00 P.M. to midnight. Moderate. Metro: U Street–Cardozo (green line).

Florida Avenue Grill, 1100 Florida Avenue NW; 265–1580. This classic, counter-and-stools (plus a few booths) neighborhood grill is lined with photos of the political and showbiz leaders who have dined in this Washington institution on "Southern-style food." It's easy to see why. Break-

---

Where to Find the Author's Favorite Places to Eat in Shaw and U Street

Diversite
1526 14th Street NW; 234–5740
(see page 146 for full listing)

HR57
1610 14th Street NW; 667–3700
(see page 147 for full listing)

U-Topia
(see page 147 for full listing)

Polly's
1342 U Street NW; 265–8385
(see page 147 for full listing)

Ben's Chili Bowl
1231 U Street NW; 667–0909
(see page 148 for full listing)

The Islander
1201 U Street; 234–4955
(see page 149 for full listing)

fasts are big here, with possibilities that range from hotcakes to omelettes and sides of scrapple, spicy half smokes, grits with redeye gravy, or all of the above. Lunch or dinner might be tasty barbecue, pork chops, or real southern fried chicken like the Colonel doesn't make. Open Tuesday through Saturday 6:00 A.M. to 9:00 P.M. Inexpensive. Metro: U Street–Cardozo (green line).

The Saloon, 1205 U Street NW; 462–2640. Located in a nicely restored 1890s vintage building, the Saloon's menu is strictly all-American, with burgers, sandwiches, and grills, but the beer list is international and includes suds from fifteen countries. The Saloon is open Tuesday through Saturday 11:30 A.M. to 1:00 A.M.; live jazz every Friday and Saturday night. Inexpensive. Metro: U Street–Cardozo (green line).

Jinny French's Southwestern Cuisine, 1940 11th Street NW; 234–8790. True to its name, this converted town house offers up Southern cooking and a few touches of Texas in a cafeteria-style setting. Open Tuesday through Thursday 9:00 A.M. to 8:00 P.M., Friday and Saturday until 9:00 P.M., Sunday until 6:00 P.M. Inexpensive. Metro: U Street–Cardozo (green line).

Indexes

Entries for Restaurants, Lodgings, Children's Sites, African-American Sites, Jewish Sites, Lincoln Sites, and House Museums appear in the special indexes beginning on page 161.

General Index

Restaurants

Lodgings

Children's Sites

African–American Sites

About the Author

Bill Whitman is a former diplomat who spent most of his career in Yugoslavia and in Italy, where he started writing about travel and food. He now lives in Washington, D.C. where he writes for major magazines, including *National Geographic Traveler, Hemispheres*, and *Forbes-FYI*. He has also written two other books, *Literary Cities of Italy*, which takes readers to the literary landmarks of Rome, Florence, and Venice, and *Wines of Virginia*, a comprehensive guide to Virginia's wines and wineries.